Somerset County

Maryland

Somerset County *Maryland*

A Brief History

Jason Rhodes

The History Press

Published by The History Press
Charleston, SC 29403
www.historypress.net

Front cover: Virginia Mae passes through Crisfield's historic Jersey Island Drawbridge in 1956. *Courtesy Scorchy Tawes.*

All photos courtesy of the author unless otherwise noted.

First published 2007

Manufactured in the United States

ISBN 978.1.59629.273.4

Library of Congress Cataloging-in-Publication Data

Rhodes, Jason.
Somerset County, Maryland : a brief history / Jason Rhodes.
p. cm.
Includes bibliographical references.
ISBN 978-1-59629-273-4 (alk. paper)
1. Somerset County (Md.)--History. I. Title.
F187.S7R48 2007
975.2'23--dc22
2007021393

Contents

Acknowledgements

Undertaking any project of this size would be impossible without assistance from many individuals dedicated to preserving the history of Somerset County. The author extends thanks to Brent Connor, Richard Crumbacker, Phil Goldsborough and Frank Rhodes for their help in researching this volume. Thanks also to Mark Bradshaw, Faye Pianka, Cindy Powell and Scorchy Tawes for providing several of the photos throughout this edition.

This book is dedicated to my sister, Carrie Rhodes.

Captain Johnny Marshall's boat and store were landmarks of Smith Island during the first half of the twentieth century. *Courtesy Mark Bradshaw.*

Chapter 1

Early Explorers and Settlements

Captain John Smith never shied away from adventure. In 1596, at about age seventeen, he left his inherited home in England to fight alongside other volunteers for Dutch independence from Spain. From there, he wandered through France and Italy before touring the Mediterranean aboard a merchant ship. Shortly thereafter, he joined the Austrian Empire in its battle against the Turks, becoming a prisoner of war in Transylvania.

By 1604, Smith was back in England, where it appeared he would stay. However, fate had other plans. Smith grew excited at talk of colonizing the New World. By winter of 1606, he had signed on with the Virginia Company, a group of 144 colonists chartered by King James I to explore the land that eventually would become the United States. Sailing from England that December, the colonists reached land May 13, 1607. They called their new home Jamestown in honor of the king.

Smith served as one of seven councilors, helping rule the new colony. However, by December 1607, about two-thirds of the colonists had died. As the council of seven became less effective, Smith emerged as the colony's leader. Leading expeditions inland in search of food, he was able to trade with Native Americans for corn. During one of these exploratory expeditions, he famously was captured by a Native American hunting party whose members took him to Chief Powhatan.

Whether Smith escaped death during his capture due to the intervention of Powhatan's young daughter, Pocahontas, or whether Powhatan released the prisoner on his own accord is a topic still debated by historians today. However, when Smith returned to Jamestown, he found his power taken by Captain Christopher Newport and Gabriel Archer, two fellow colonists.

Regardless of who was in command, Jamestown was still in dire straits. A lack of food and shelter continued to threaten the colony's survival. More heroic accounts of Smith's journey say he decided to take matters into his own hands, searching for a new food supply and salt to preserve what food still existed. Others suggest he simply left the colony in an attempt to escape the pressures he faced as a former leader toppled from power.

What is certain is that in June 1608, three months before regaining his position in Jamestown and sixteen months before losing it again and returning to England, he gathered a crew, boarded the ship *Phoenix* and set sail on one of the most important exploratory voyages in U.S. history. Exploring the Potomac and Rappahannock Rivers and the Chesapeake Bay, Smith drew the earliest known map of the bay.

Among the areas chronicled during this journey were the Russell Isles, a group of islands in the Chesapeake Bay that Smith named after a doctor onboard the ship. While two of the Russell Isles—today known as Tangier and Watts—eventually became part of Virginia, the third, later named Smith Island in honor of early landowner Henry Smith, would be part of Maryland. With this discovery, Smith registered the first confirmed sighting of what today is Somerset County.

However, that is not to say Smith was the first European ever to see a portion of what would become Somerset. In 1498, Italian explorer John Cabot, leading an expedition on behalf of King Edward V of England, spoke of seeing a coastline that likely was the modern-day Worcester County, a part of early Somerset.

Likewise, Italian explorer Giovanni da Verrazano sailed into the area in 1524, leading an expedition on behalf of King Francis I of France. Aboard the ship *Dauphine*, he and his fifty-man crew explored many parts of what is today Eastern Shore Virginia before turning back upon reaching a portion of the Pocomoke River too marshy to navigate. It is believed da Verrazano made it as far as Public Landing, another portion of early Somerset, before turning back to the mouth of the Chesapeake.

Nearly eight decades later, in 1603, Bartholomew Gilbert sailed to the New World from England aboard his fifty-ton ship, *Elizabeth*, in an expedition to locate survivors of Sir Walter Raleigh's "lost colony" settlement. Making their way toward what is now North Carolina, Gilbert and his crew hit a storm and sought refuge in the Chesapeake Bay. Anchoring in Bullock's Channel, between the mainland and what is now Smith Island, a four-man crew set out on land in search of fresh water. Only two returned. Gilbert and another crewman were killed by Native Americans, their deaths ending the mission to find Raleigh's survivors.

Despite this incident, Native Americans in the area were not universally unfriendly. In fact, written accounts largely portray the region's Native American tribes as cooperative with European explorers. Records from 1620 recount a trading session between the Manokin and visiting Europeans at a Native American village along the south bank of Manokin Creek in what is now Princess Anne. Explorers came to call this area "Indian Neck."

While early trading, like that done in Jamestown, was for survival, the Europeans quickly discovered they could make money from these sessions. Prior to settling in the Manokin area in 1661, Virginian John Westlock established a trading post on Kings Creek in what is today Princess Anne, earning the area the early name "Trading Branch." There, he and other Europeans traded beads, blankets, bows, hatchets, cloth, bells, mirrors, roanoke (conch shells) and peake (cockleshells) for pelts and furs that could be shipped back to England and sold at a huge profit.

Most valuable among these items for the Europeans were skins of animals bountiful on the Eastern Shore at the time, including beavers, otters, wildcats, bears, foxes, minks, wolves, raccoons, elk, deer, rabbits and muskrats. The Native Americans, in the meantime, reportedly were especially enamored of the peake, which often garnered more furs than any other item the Europeans had to trade.

Thanks to the efforts of early expeditions like that of the Virginia Company, King James I had claimed a large portion of North America's eastern coast in the name of England. This was good news for the kingdom, but even better news for the king's closest associates, many of whom were deeded sections of that property to settle as British colonies.

One such associate was George Calvert, the first Baron of Baltimore and the king's principal secretary of state. Though Calvert gave up his governmental position to rejoin the Catholic Church at a time when Protestants ruled England, the king still held him in high enough regard to approve his request for a land grant in the New World. In fact, the king even granted Calvert princely rights in the new colony, allowing him to collect taxes, make laws and distribute land to anyone he saw fit.

An investor in the Virginia Company, Calvert had long been a supporter of colonization. However, he passed away in 1632 before seeing his dream of governing his own colony come to fruition. The charter for the colony, by then named Maryland ("Terra Maria") after Queen Henrietta Maria, was passed on to his son, Cecilius, Lord Baltimore. Cecilius recruited his brother, Leonard, to lead the first expedition to the colony.

Two ships, *Ark* and *Dove*, left Cowes on the Isle of Wight on November 22, 1633, reaching Maryland more than four months later on March 25, 1634. Acquiring land from the Yaocomico, Leonard and his 233 passengers were successful in establishing St. Mary's, the fourth permanent European settlement in the New World.

However, this success came with a price. Early settlers disagreed with the Calverts' feudalistic governance, which led to the creation of a colonial assembly in February 1635. Within three years, the assembly stripped the Calverts of their rights to form an individual government. Legislative rights were transferred to the assembly, and Maryland was governed under the laws of England.

In 1644, Leonard Calvert seized a trading post founded by Virginian William Claiborne in the area now known as Kent Island. In an attempt to regain the post, Claiborne led an uprising of Maryland Protestants, uniting them against Calvert's Catholicism. Because most of the two hundred laborers that had established the colony were Protestant, he had little trouble outnumbering Calvert, who fled to Virginia.

The Calverts had seen this type of religious conflict as a potential problem since George was first granted the charter. Because of this, the colony had no official established religion. Furthermore, they instituted a "liberty of conscience" policy that banned no Christian religion within the colony. Clearly, they discovered, this was not enough.

Raising an army of Catholic supporters, Leonard returned to St. Mary's and regained power until passing the governorship to Thomas Greene in 1647. Maryland became one of the few Catholic regions in the colonies. It also attracted many English exiles who had been persecuted for non-Protestant beliefs in their home country. In 1649, Lord Baltimore made this type of religious tolerance official with the Maryland Toleration Act, sometimes seen as a precursor to the first amendment to the U.S. Constitution.

Despite the influx of English immigrants to Maryland, the colony remained underpopulated, especially on the Eastern Shore. Lord Baltimore began to fear if he did not have settlers on this land soon, it would be absorbed into Virginia.

In a letter, he ordered Governor Josias Fendall to "encourage some English as soon as you can to take up such land as shall be due them in our said province on or near the bounds of our province on that tract of land which is commonly called the Eastern Shore lying between the bay of Chesapeake and the sea for the better publication and remembrance of the bounds between Virginia and Maryland and prevention of controversies which may otherwise hereafter happen between the inhabitants of Virginia and those of our province."

As of March 1657, no permanent settlements had been registered between the Choptank River and what is today the Maryland-Virginia state line. However, the Maryland Toleration Act was about to pay off in a way Lord Baltimore likely never dreamed.

In March 1659, the Virginia General Assembly passed a law prohibiting Quakers from entering that colony, claiming them to be an "unreasonable and turbulent sort of people who daily gather together unlawful assemblies of people, teaching lies, miracles, false visions, prophecies and doctrines tending to disturb the peace, disorganize society and destroy all law and government and religion."

Quakers already living in Virginia were appalled. When protests failed, they sought new places to live. A number wrote Lord Baltimore to request admittance into Maryland. On November 6, 1661, Maryland Governor Phillip Calvert, Leonard's son, published an official invitation to all displaced Virginia Quakers to relocate to Maryland, where their religious beliefs would be accepted with open arms.

Less ingeniously, Lord Baltimore also banned non-Maryland residents from trading with Native Americans on Maryland soil, causing potential problems for Virginia merchants who depended on regional Native American trade to continue their livelihoods. With these two incentives, the Eastern Shore's underpopulation problem vanished practically overnight.

By 1662, Maryland recorded fifty taxable households between the Manokin and Big Annemessex Rivers. As many as two hundred people are believed to have moved to that region that year. Among them were Stephen Horsey, a former Virginia General Assembly burgess for Northampton County who, while not a Quaker, was an advocate for religious tolerance. Quickly taking a liking to Horsey, Lord Baltimore made him a commissioner, allowing him to grant Maryland land to other Virginia emigrants. He later became the first high sheriff and chief judge of Somerset County.

Another Virginia emigrant of note was Ambrose Dixon, who also settled on the south side of the Big Annemessex. His 850-acre plantation—Dixon's Choice, near what is now Marion Station—was the first Quaker meeting place on the Eastern Shore and eventually became Maryland's first sanctioned burial ground. Though elected as a Somerset County representative to the Maryland General Assembly in 1670, no record of his actually attending the assembly exists.

Nearly all known Quakers who settled in the Big Annemessex area during this time went on to serve in public office. Henry Boston, who lived on a 750-acre plantation next door to Dixon and known as "Boston Town," was a volunteer member of the Commission of the Peace, a forerunner to organized law enforcement in the area. George Johnson, a former Virginia merchant, also was a volunteer with the Commission of the Peace. He inherited the position of high sheriff from Horsey in 1668.

Another neighbor, Edmund Beauchamp, came to the area at the request of Governor Charles Calvert to become clerk of court for the region that would become Somerset County, a job he held for a quarter century. Beauchamp married Dixon's daughter, Sarah, and they lived on a three-hundred-acre plantation, named Contention, at the head of the Big Annemessex.

Many of the settlers in the area that would become southern Somerset County came to escape religious persecution. In contrast, most who settled in the northern region, between the Manokin River and Back Creek, came to take advantage of land availability. As Virginia filled with colonists, Maryland became a popular alternative for realty.

Among the most notable settlers in this area was Randall Revell, a wine cooper who owned a combined 7,300 acres of land among his three plantations: Arrococo, Revell's Grove and Double Purchase. The community of Revells Neck, where Double Purchase once stood, is named in his honor today. A Maryland commissioner with land-granting rights, he made one of the first formal arrangements known between settlers and Native Americans in the region.

In 1662, Revell made an agreement with the emperor of the Nanticokes to supply six matchcoats for each plantation sold by tribe members, pay one matchcoat for each runaway slave the tribe's members helped return, call a truce to murder and theft, arrange formal trading opportunities and ensure any European entering Native American land had a letter of authority to pass.

However, his reign was short-lived. From 1662 to 1663, Revell served as chief resident official of the Manokin settlement. In 1663 he was removed from that position, and his powers as a commissioner were revoked shortly thereafter and given instead to Stephen Horsey. This sudden change of events likely was the consequence of his suspected dealings with Colonel Edmund Scarborough, a Virginia loyalist also given Maryland commissioner rights by Governor Charles Calvert as a show of good faith.

The brother of King James I's personal physician, Sir Charles Scarborough, the colonel was appointed to surveyor-general and treasurer of the Virginia colony, becoming one of the few non-governors in the region to report directly to the king. A proud Virginian, he made it his life's ambition to add as much land as possible to the Virginia colony.

One of Scarborough's earliest schemes was to claim that Watkins Point, named as the boundary line between Maryland and Virginia, was not at the mouth of the Annemessex River, but rather at the mouth of the Wicomico River, thirty miles north. Using Captain John Smith's original Chesapeake Bay map, he pointed out Smith had named the Pocomoke River "Wighcomoco." He insisted Smith's "Wighcomoco" was merely a colloquial interpretation of "Wicomico." In reality, Wighcomoco was a Native American settlement on the Pocomoke River. The Wicomico River did not appear on Smith's map.

Nonetheless, Scarborough insisted the residents of the Annemessex settlement pay tithes to Virginia. When they refused, he arrested their leaders and attempted to claim their plantations in the name of Virginia.

He employed different tactics at the Manokin settlement. In Virginia, he led attacks against the historically peaceful Assateagues, making many of its members distrustful of the Europeans. He warned the Manokin settlers of the "savage" Native American attacks they would encounter, using the Assateague battles as examples. At the same time, Virginia emigrant John Nuttall was sent to agitate the local Native Americans, telling them the settlers at Manokin would treat them the same way Scarborough's men treated the Assateagues.

Scarborough offered the settlers protection if they would agree their homes were part of Virginia. The Manokin settlers also requested protection against members of the Annemessex settlement, who had tried to make the Manokin residents wary of Scarborough's promises by warning them the Maryland government would take action if they attempted to cede from the colony.

Upon hearing of the situation, Governor Charles Calvert met with Virginia Governor William Berkeley, and the two formed a commission to determine the Maryland-Virginia boundary line once and for all. However, before that commission could meet, Scarborough and forty-four men marched on the Annemessex settlement, attempting to capture it by force. Once again, he failed.

The two governors appointed a second commission, which met in March 1664. However, without Virginia's official surveyors present, no legal decision was reached. Scarborough attempted to mark a tree at the mouth of the Wicomico River as "Watkins Point." Once again, Charles Calvert complained, this time sending his chancellor, Philip Calvert, to meet with Berkeley. They agreed the two colonies should live peaceably until a decision could be reached.

That decision came in 1668, when Philip Calvert and Scarborough, forming a two-man commission, met at the real Watkins Point under the direction of the colonies' respective governors. Scarborough conceded what Watkins Point was indeed at the mouth of the Annemessex. The boundary line was deemed official—at least for a while.

Several years later, other surveyors reviewed the line determined by Calvert and Scarborough and found it was run incorrectly. Some twenty-three square miles of property legally belonging to Maryland erroneously had been placed in Virginia, and Virginia had granted rights to thirty-three thousand acres of it. The land was returned to Maryland—including five thousand acres belonging to Scarborough.

Whether he truly did have underhanded dealings with Scarborough, Revell redeemed himself in the eyes of Maryland's governing officials, becoming the high sheriff of the area in 1670. He also cemented his place in Maryland history as the first person on record suggesting that a county be formed to encompass Annemessex, Manokin and their outlying areas.

Following Revell's term as chief resident officer of Manokin, Charles Calvert transferred the power to another land-granting commissioner, John Elzey. An emigrant

The ornate brick mansion now associated with Make Peace remains as one of the oldest homes in Somerset County in the twenty-first century.

from Accomack County, Virginia, Elzey owned three plantations in the settlement: the 300-acre Sweetwood, the 250-acre Erlindy and 1,000-acre Almodington. Regarded as the only completely honest original commissioner at Manokin, his leadership was a large factor in keeping the settlement from succumbing to Scarborough's advances. However, it was also short-lived. Elzey died in office in 1664.

Other notable early settlers at Manokin included Will Thorne, John Odber and William Bosman. Living on the 600-acre plantation, Thornton, Thorne was the first captain of the Commission of the Peace. Odber, also a Commission of the Peace captain, helped form an army to ward off attacks from Native Americans. He lost his rank in 1664 and was killed by a member of the Wicomicos three years later. Bosman owned the 1,200-acre More and Case It plantation and later was appointed a land-granting commissioner.

Meanwhile, some settlers turned their attention to areas off the mainland. In 1657, records indicate the first inhabitants on the island that is today Smith Island. Two somewhat contradictory stories exist as to why settlers chose to live on the island at that particular time. One story is that they were dissenters, either from one of Lord Baltimore's established settlements or from the Jamestown colony, who sought to establish a settlement of their own.

Another story is that a farmer sought to raise livestock in a haven safe from Native American attacks and wild animal predators found on the mainland. According to that story, the first settlers on the island were farmhands hired to help raise the livestock. Regardless, some of the first names registered on the island—Bradshaw, Evans and Tyler—are names that largely remain there today. It is also believed many of these first residents were not only of English descent, but Welsh, as well, helping account for the unique accent still found on the island.

By 1666, the push to create a county on Maryland's lower Eastern Shore was growing, and so were the number of plantations established in the area. On February 10 of that year, the three-hundred-acre plantation Emmesox was surveyed for Benjamin Somers (or Summers, in some references), another former Virginia Quaker, near Annemessex.

Several days later, the plantation Make Peace was surveyed for John Roach on a parcel of land originally patented in 1663 outside Annemessex. It was on this ground that Native Americans in the area met with early settlers to hold peace talks. While conventional wisdom says this is the activity that gave the home its name, a legend has remained that the building actually was named in honor of a Native American princess, Manoka, who became romantically involved with one of its early owners.

Roughly translated, the legend says, "Manoka" was the Native American equivalent of "Make Peace" in the English tongue. Lower Somerset folklorist Gus Ward popularized the legend in his 1930 book *Down in Maryland*, though the author offered no background on the story's origin.

Regardless of how it received its name, the ornate brick mansion now associated with Make Peace remains as one of the oldest homes in Somerset County in the twenty-first century.

Chapter 2

Somerset Begins

With his boundary lines now firmly established, Lord Baltimore was finally ready to act on the suggestion of Randall Revell and others to officially designate his lower Eastern Shore holdings an official county in the colony of Maryland. On August 22, 1666, he signed an Order in Council, decreeing that all land between the Wicomico River and Watkins Point be incorporated as the County of Somerset. In naming the county, he continued the tradition of branding territories in honor of family members and English nobles, in this case Lady Mary Somerset, sister of Lord Baltimore's wife, Anne Calvert (née Anne Arundel).

Lord Baltimore wasted no time offering incentives to draw even more people to his new county. That same year he authorized Governor Charles Calvert to make all Eastern Shore land adjacent to the Atlantic Ocean available to anyone who wished to settle there. Their rent would be only one shilling per year for fifty acres. Though the incentive went a bit beyond its boundaries, encroaching on land that was later surveyed as part of Delaware, it was successful in populating the Eastern Shore's Atlantic seaboard in what is today Worcester County.

The population was also growing from within. Records show that Margaret Mitchell, daughter of George and Isabel Mitchell of Great Monie, was the first child born in the newly created Somerset County, on August 23, 1666. Great Monie was one of several settlements established in the area in the 1600s, both formally and informally, as more settlers were attracted to the lower Eastern Shore. During the next few decades, they settled new parts of the shore, as well. The first land grant in the area now known as Deal Island was issued to a man named John Laws in 1676.

Another area that grew during this time was Smith Island, named in honor of Henry Smith, who patented the thousand-acre plantation Pitchcroft on the island on June 3, 1679. A notable early resident of Somerset County, Smith moved to the Coulbourn Creek area from Accomack County, Virginia, in 1669. He later lived on the White House plantation on the Manokin River, where he died in 1702. Interestingly, there are no records to indicate Smith ever actually lived on his namesake island. Most likely he purchased the land as an investment property or used it, as perhaps its earliest settlers did, to raise livestock in a safe environment with the help of indentured servants.

While areas like Smith Island grew, one of Somerset's earliest settlements, Manokin, was fading. By 1666, only one taxpayer, John Winder, was registered in the original Manokin settlement. Moving to Somerset from Nansemond County, Virginia, in 1665, he settled on Back Creek on a two-hundred-acre plantation he named Winder's Purchase. He also owned a three-hundred-acre plantation, Kikatan's Choice.

Favored by Maryland officials, he was named a commissioner of the peace, serving from 1665 to 1666, and an early member of the Somerset County Court. He also served as one of Somerset's first justices of the peace. He moved to a plantation on the Wicomico River about 1670, and served as an officer in an ongoing calvary expedition against the Nanticokes from 1678 until his death in 1698, enforcing peace between the Native Americans and new settlers. Colonel William Stevens, leader of the calvary in Somerset and Dorchester Counties, held a Native American treaty meeting at Winder's Wicomico River home in 1687.

Stevens himself was a notable early Somerset County resident, moving to the area in late 1664. Serving as a commissioner of the peace from 1665 to 1666, he was seen as one of the most honorable to hold the position. This high regard made him a natural choice to serve as the first judge of the Somerset County Court—a position he held for twenty-two years.

Convening on September 4, 1666, the first act of this new court was to issue marriage licenses, or "bands of matrimony," to John O'Kee and Mary Vincent, both of Manokin, and to Thomas Tull of Annemessex and Mary Minshell of Marumsco. Records show Winder married O'Kee and Vincent the next month. Justice of the Peace George Johnson similarly married Tull and Minshell.

Comprised of Justices Stevens, Winder, William Thorne and Henry Boston, the first Somerset County Court assumed many of the powers originally granted to the governor of Maryland. During its second session, January 17, 1667, at the home of Thomas Poole in Manokin, the justices laid out plans for infrastructure to grow the county in short order.

By the end of that session, county officials had orders to begin construction of Somerset's inaugural highway, from the home of Captain Goyeders on the Pocomoke River to Marumsco to Coulbourn Creek to Watkins Point. The court determined Somerset officials would also construct the county's first courthouse.

That first court building was constructed 1675 in Sommerton, on part of twenty acres of land on the Manokin River that Lord Baltimore purchased from Randall Revell in hopes of turning it into Somerset's county seat. In 1683, justices determined a new courthouse was needed. They contracted with Henry Smith to construct the new building on a tract of land called Webley, near modern-day Princess Anne, at a cost of twelve thousand pounds of tobacco. In 1694, the courthouse was moved to Dividing Creek, near the Pocomoke River, in an attempt to centralize court activities to accommodate the county's growing Atlantic population.

Justices also took time during the 1667 session to determine community boundaries throughout the county. These official communities were known as "hundreds," as was the tradition in England at the time. A "hundred" in England had a population large enough to send at least one hundred men into the armed forces if called, though that was not necessarily the case in some of Somerset County's hundreds. The first hundreds in the county were Pocomoke, Manokin, Great Monie, Little Monie, Wicomico and Annamessex. Four more—Nanticoke, Bogerte Morton, Mattapany and Baltimore—later followed.

In England, each hundred was eligible to send a representative to Parliament. In Maryland, most hundreds could send a representative to the General Assembly in St. Mary's. However, since Somerset's population during its first General Assembly session did not warrant a representative from each hundred, colony officials asked the county's early residents to choose only two. Under an election overseen by George Johnson, they chose Colonel Stevens and William Horsey. However, in the end, it was decided only Stevens should go to St. Mary's, representing the entire county. The decision puzzled colony officials, and no explanation remains on record as to why Somerset leaders settled on only half the number of representatives to which they were entitled.

Nonetheless, colony leaders adored Stevens as much, if not more, than his county constituents. Following his first year at the General Assembly, he returned with much favor in 1678 and became a member of the Governor's Privy Council the next year. When Governor Calvert had to take a leave of office in 1864 to return to England, leaving his underaged son, Benedict, to take over duties as the colony's leader, Stevens was named one of several deputy governors to advise the boy.

While Stevens made great strides as a leader at both the county and colony levels, perhaps his greatest achievements were in the religious realm. Born into the Church of England, Stevens, like many early Somerset settlers, was tolerant of all religions. He signed documents supporting Catholicism and represented the Quakers alongside all other religions in his duties as a member of the General Assembly.

However, he was not completely satisfied with the county's religious makeup. He urged the Irish Presbyterian Church to send a missionary to this new county. As early as 1680, a small group of Somerset Presbyterians was said to have been meeting at a house in Manokin. In 1683 Williams received his wish, as Francis Makemie, ordained by the Presbytery of Laggan, was sent to Somerset County.

Makemie established the first—or second, depending on the source—Presbyterian church in the American colonies in Stevens's home community of Rehobeth and built a meetinghouse there in 1706 on land given to him by Stevens. In 1684 (1683 by some accounts), he also established a congregation in the Somerset County community of Snow Hill, building a meetinghouse on land Stevens owned there. This site also has been claimed as the first Presbyterian church in the colonies. Between 1683 and 1686, he helped bring recognition to the Presbyterians of Princess Anne, leading to the establishment of Manokin Presbyterian Church.

From his Rehobeth base, Makemie traveled the colonies, from New England to North Carolina, raising awareness of the Presbyterian faith. In 1706, he brought leaders from several Presbyterian backgrounds together to form the Presbytery of Philadelphia, an event widely considered to be the birth of American Presbyterianism.

Though he had a license to preach in Virginia, where he owned land, and in Maryland, Makemie did not have a license to preach in New York. This led to his arrest

Francis Makemie established Rehobeth Presbyterian Church, the first—or second, depending on the source—Presbyterian church in the American colonies, about 1863. The historic building associated with the church is seen here in 1975.

Between 1683 and 1686, Makemie helped bring recognition to the Presbyterians of Princess Anne, leading to the establishment of Manokin Presbyterian Church, seen here in the 1960s.

by Lord Cornbury, governor of New York, in May 1707. After spending six weeks in jail, he was acquitted that June on the basis of the English Toleration Act of 1689. His trial is still considered a landmark case in favor of religious freedom throughout the United States. However, Makemie did not have long to savor his victory, passing away the following summer.

By the time Makemie arrived, Rehobeth was a thriving community. This was not by accident. While Lord Baltimore encouraged settlers to help establish all parts of Maryland, he felt strongly that each county should have certain areas of concentrated growth to help facilitate trade by establishing ports of entry along the state's waterways. There, merchants could load goods onto boats for shipping or receive the latest shipments of goods from other colonies and even Europe.

Lord Baltimore named five such ports to be established in Somerset County: Rehobeth and Snow Hill on the Pocomoke River, Sommerton on the Manokin River, Horsey's Landing south of Coulbourn Creek in Annemessex, and a fifth port on the Wicomico River on a point opposite what is now Whitehaven. Snow Hill became especially important as a colonial port in the next three decades. In 1694, it was established as a royal port, exporting cypress lumber (for shipbuilding) and tobacco to England.

As Somerset County's ports and hundreds grew, so did their need for services settlers had found readily available in many parts of England. The first teacher on record in Somerset County is Mrs. John Avery of Marumsco, who agreed to teach the children of her neighbor, Mary Barnable, in exchange for a two-year-old calf. Her husband had to go to court to claim the payment when Barnable died before the lessons were completed. Another early Somerset teacher, James Osborne, taught two children, Thomas and Susannah Walker, in 1685 for payment of 1,500 pounds of tobacco.

In the next few decades, education became even more important not just in Somerset County, but in Maryland as a whole. In 1694, Governor Frances Nicholson asked the General Assembly to pass an act creating a public school system. Passed two years later, the act established the colony's first school tax on furs, beef and bacon.

The next year, items taxable for the education fund included bear, beaver, otter, wildcat, fox, mink, wolf, raccoon, elk, deer and muskrat skins. This caused a certain degree of controversy in Somerset County, where these pelts were popular items of trade. Eventually, the tax grew to include imports as well, focusing on everything from material goods shipped from Europe to slaves and servants brought into the colony from Africa and Ireland.

Despite paying education taxes for decades, the people of Somerset never saw a formal school in their own county until 1726, when a schoolhouse was built on the Manokin River between Kings and Jones Creeks. Schools were required only when an area's school-aged population numbered one hundred or more. Somerset's earliest school trustees were John Huett and Colonel Frances Jenkins. The earliest classes focused on Latin, Greek and writing.

About the same time colonists began thinking about education, religion was becoming more important in Somerset. The Church of England emerged as a popular religion in the county about 1680. The first Roman Catholics in the area came around 1700.

Makemie helped popularize Presbyterianism from 1683 on, and the Quakers and English Catholics were part of the Eastern Shore practically from the beginning.

The Quaker movement gained ground in Somerset in 1672. George Fox, founder of the Society of Friends—the basis for the Quaker religion—ran aground in the county while sailing in a storm on February 2 of that year. Finding a friendly populace, much of which was already Quaker, he spent about a month in Somerset, hosting meetings in communities along the Annemessex, Manokin and Wicomico Rivers.

Despite their religious faith, many Somerset Quakers at that time had never seen a true ordained Quaker minister. Fox's draw was so large that many communities temporarily disbanded gatherings at their traditional meetinghouses in favor of barns to accommodate the number in attendance. He also visited several Native American leaders in the region, including Emperor Wynicasso, King Dunhill of the Pocomokes and the queen of the Assateagues, recorded alternately as Weowocomico and Weocomoconus.

While all reportedly welcomed Fox with open arms, they were a bit mystified by his style of dress. In Europe, men of the cloth wore traditional garments. Preaching in the colonies, however, Fox dressed the same as most colonial men. This drew the attention of many of the county's agnostic residents, some of whom are said to have converted after witnessing his meetings.

Other Quaker ministers followed in early Somerset, including Thomas Chalkley, brought to Annemessex by settler Thomas Everndon in 1689, and Thomas Story, who came to Somerset from Philadelphia about 1702. Under his guidance, the Court of Somerset granted permission for three more Quakers, George Truitt, Richard Waters and Levin Denwood, to hold religious meetings in their homes in 1704.

Almost immediately after Fox's departure, the Court of Somerset decreed there would be regular preaching by a representative of the Presbyterian church at four locations in the county: Colonel Stevens's home in Rehobeth on the first Sunday of each month, Daniel Curtis's on the Annemessex River each second Sunday, Christopher Nutter's on the Manokin River each third Sunday and Thomas Roe's on the Wicomico River each fourth Sunday. Robert Maddox was the appointed preacher.

Prior to 1680, the Reverend Thomas Teackle, minister of the Church of England, also made occasional visits to preach in Somerset. That was not enough for Captain Thomas Walker, who stated in his will, "I give to the first Protestant minister that shall hereafter come from England to live in this county towards his transportation one thousand pounds of good tobacco."

John Huett, the same man who later became one of the county's first school trustees, heeded the call. Moving to Somerset in 1680, he buried Captain Walker, who was remembered not only for his generosity in advancing the Church of England, but as a Somerset sheriff, naval officer, trader, merchant and magistrate.

Walker's tobacco offer may have helped attract Huett to Somerset County, but it did not make the preacher's cause any easier. Without a formal church, Huett ministered door-to-door for fifteen years as the county's only permanent Church of England minister. Traveling primarily by water, he gave sermons in communities along the Nanticoke, Wicomico, Monie, Manokin, Annamessex and Pocomoke Rivers.

He also made religious inroads with the local Native American tribes. Records show that he baptized at least one Native American as John Puckham at Great Monie Creek. The Native American allegedly took "John" as his Christian name in honor of Huett. Indeed, several of the Native Americans from that era listed in Somerset tax and judicial records have English names as part of their own, including Robin John of the Pocomoke and Richard James of the Monie. Other Native American names found from records of this era include Katuckcuweitick of the Manokin, Mackismat of the Wicomico and Machacopah of the Pocomoke.

In the late 1600s, politics in England helped shape the future of Somerset. As leadership of the Maryland colony was taken away from Charles Calvert—who assumed the Lord Baltimore title in 1675—and assumed by King George I, it became an official royal colony. In 1692, under this royal command, the Maryland General Assembly voted to make the Church of England the official religion of Maryland.

With this vote, churches became more organized. In Somerset, the church was divided into four parishes: Somerset (serving the Manokin and Monie River communities at Somerset Church), Coventry (serving the Pocomoke and Annemessex River communities at Pocomoke Church), Stepney (serving the Wicomico and Nanticoke River communities at Huett's home) and All Hallows (serving the Bogerte Morton and Mattapany communities in Snow Hill).

These early "churches" likely were the designated homes of parishioners, except at All Hallows, where open-air services sometimes were held, and Coventry, which may have used Colonel Stevens's property at one point. During this time, tithes were collected to support the church, a practice which eventually led to the construction of church buildings in each parish. Records show that early on in this new parish system, 304 tithable men in Somerset Parish paid 12,100 pounds of tobacco to the church, while 369 men in Coventry paid 14,760 pounds.

Shortly after the first churches, colonists also constructed "chapels of ease"—smaller meeting buildings that were easier to reach during the sometimes harsh winter months. The first of these in Stepney Parish was Goddard's Chapel on the south side of Wicomico Creek, about five minutes north of modern-day Princess Anne.

Huett himself was rewarded for his earlier efforts in promoting the Church of England on the Eastern Shore. In 1692, he was elected as one of Somerset's representatives to the General Assembly. However, legislators balked at having a minister have a hand in creating colonial policy. Instead, they appointed him chaplain of the first Maryland General Assembly session as a royal colony. He continued to serve the people of Somerset until his death in 1698.

For decades while sending representatives to the state legislative seat of St. Mary's—then Annapolis after the capital moved in 1695—Somerset itself had no county seat. Sommerton had never taken off the way Lord Baltimore had hoped it would, and all thoughts of maintaining that area as the county seat died when Maryland became a royal colony.

In 1732, a group of men approached Captain David Brown with the idea of rectifying the county seat problem. Brown, a prominent landowner in the county, owned several vast parcels of land along the Manokin River. These men asked him to sell twenty-five acres of it to them with the idea of creating a county seat in the middle of Somerset so it would be equally accessible to all. Brown relented, agreeing to sell twenty-five acres in the area known as Beckford, south of the Manokin Bridge. The Somerset County Court recognized the importance of transportation in this area early on, ordering construction of the bridge in 1689.

That same year Brown sold the land, the Maryland General Assembly decreed all but one of those twenty-five acres would be developed into a new town in Somerset County, named in honor of Princess Anne, the oldest daughter of King George II of England. A surveyor was hired to lay out the new town at a cost of four hundred pounds of tobacco.

Princess Anne Town was laid out in a block system, with a grid of four east-west streets intersecting a grid of four north-south streets. The town boundary to the north was Front Street, today known as Water Street, paralleling the Manokin River. Other east-west streets, laid out north from Front Street, were Broad Street, Prince William Street and Upper Alley (now Washington Street).

Bridge Street, now Somerset Avenue, was the main entry point into Princess Anne Town, connecting with the Manokin Bridge. Immediately west was Upper Alley, now Beechwood Avenue. On the east side of town was Low Alley (now Beckford Avenue), followed to the west by New Market Street (now Church Street). Most of the original streets were seventy-four feet long.

Once the town's streets and boundaries were laid out, it was time to designate lots. Thirty lots were surveyed and construction stipulations set forth. Anyone purchasing a lot in Princess Anne had eighteen months to build on the property or lose his claim to the lot without restitution. The main building on each lot was to have a footprint of at least four hundred square feet and contain at least one brick chimney. Those owning the lots were ordered to pay one penny each year as a tribute to the county's lord proprietor.

One of the earliest lot designations was not for private residence, but for a new county jail. It was constructed at the intersection of Bridge and Broad Streets in 1737.

A second prominent Eastern Shore town was chartered on the Wicomico River in Somerset County on August 8, 1732. Though it would take more than two centuries, this town, Salisbury, would grow to become perhaps the most prosperous on the entire lower Shore by the late twentieth century.

As Somerset's population grew, its Native American population became more and more displaced. By 1686, the Pocomoke nation had been driven from its original settlement at Pocomoke to a new settlement called Aquintica and from there to a third settlement on the Pocomoke River called Askiminokonson, near where Snow Hill exists today. Some historians believe by this time, several displaced Pocomokes and Annamessex had banded together at Askiminokonson. Pocomokes and Assateagues also lived at the adjacent Queponqua settlement, west of Basket Switch.

Despite this displacement, most Native American tribes largely remained friendly with the English settlers. Peace treaties were signed with the Pocomokes, Annamessex, Assateagues, Manokins, Wicomicos and Nanticokes, though how effective those treaties were with the latter two tribes is open to debate. Settlers remained wary of the Nanticokes due to their perceived role as gatekeepers to Native American communities outside Maryland. The Wicomicos defended their land rights more vigorously than many of the other Eastern Shore Maryland tribes.

Indeed, where most run-ins between Native Americans and settlers prior to the 1660s had to do with minor trade disputes or small raids on established plantations, land rights became a major factor in negative dealings with Native Americans throughout much of the last half of the seventeenth century. According to county tax records, by 1665, settlers had claimed 42,310 acres in Somerset County. By 1690, that number had risen to 210,980.

Somerset was growing, all right. However, in the opinions of some, it was growing a little too much.

Chapter 3

A County Divided

In 1742, Somerset officials received word that Native Americans planned to stage a full-scale attack against the county. Most suspected the attack would come from the Assateague Empire, which Maryland no longer recognized. This lack of official recognition placed severe restrictions on the tribe's freedoms.

In reality, Somerset officials had no reason to fear the Assateagues. A peaceable tribe, many emigrated north to band with the Susquehanna nation. Eventually, the Somerset leaders learned it was the Nanticoke nation that was planning the attack. Regardless, it did not emerge.

What Somerset leaders likely did not realize, however, was that the tables were about to be turned. For nearly a decade, they had been encroaching on land that once belonged to the Native Americans. On December 10, 1742, Lord Baltimore Charles Calvert, who assumed leadership of the Maryland colony when the English government returned power to the Calvert family in 1715, created a new county from Somerset's easternmost section.

He named it Worcester in honor of Edward Somerset, fourth Earl of Worcester. This division encompassed not only all of modern-day Worcester County, but part of today's Wicomico County, as well. The original dividing line between Somerset and Worcester remains today as Division Street in Salisbury.

Lord Baltimore hoped this division would help solve logistical problems caused by the locations of major settlements in the original Somerset County. Settlers along the Atlantic Ocean, he thought, were too far removed geographically from those at the county's southernmost point, Annamessex. With two separate counties, meetings and services could be better centralized than they could with one large county.

Having lost their most prosperous port, Snow Hill, to Worcester County, Somerset officials were in earnest need of a true county seat. Perhaps for the first time truly embraced the idea of giving that distinction to Princess Anne Town. The area soon thrived.

One early homestead in Princess Anne was built on Lot 3 of the original lots as early as 1743. It existed on the site of the home now known as the Charles Jones house, across the street from the first courthouse built in Princess Anne, also built in 1743. The original home is thought to have burned prior to the mid-1770s. Jones bought the lot in

1782 and erected the current structure. Another early settlement was Lot 4, owned by Heber Whittingham prior to his death in 1750.

In 1751, John Bell purchased Lots 15 and 16 at a total cost of forty shillings. The next year, he sold Lot 15, now with a house, to Henry Waggaman, who in turn sold it to John Done in 1755. Improvements made to the property by new owner Zadock Long in 1797 became the basis for the Washington Hotel, which still stands on Somerset Avenue.

Built just a few years after the Bell purchase, around 1755, was the William Geddes house on Lot 7, constructed after Geddes purchased the lot from Heber Whittingham's son, Samuel. Still a fixture of Princess Anne today, this home is also known as Tunstall Cottage, as some early researchers speculated the home belonged to Captain John Tunstall. In truth, Tunstall did own three lots in Princess Anne, but never built upon them, instead seeing them as investment properties.

Two of Somerset's historic church buildings also began life during this time. By 1764, the meetinghouse of the Manokin Quakers had fallen into disrepair. The next year, the congregation paid six hundred pounds for the construction of Manokin Presbyterian Church at the site of the former home of Christopher Nutter.

Similarly, those worshiping at the King's Mill Chapel of Ease in the Somerset Parish of the Church of England found conditions there less than desirable and petitioned the Maryland General Assembly for permission to construct a new church in Princess Anne. On February 17, 1767, the congregation purchased Lots 27 and 28 from Robert Geddes for twenty-eight pounds. During the next six years, Levin Ballard undertook construction of the new building, St. Andrew's Episcopal Church. Interior construction was taking place at least by 1770, when a call went out for volunteers to build the church's pulpit. Its pews were installed in late 1773.

Education once again became an important aspect of Somerset County life. In 1723, the Maryland General Assembly passed the Academy Act that paved the way for boarding schools, or academies, in the colony. Somerset received its first, appropriately named Somerset Academy, in fall 1767. The eighty-student private school was situated on Back Creek, roughly eight miles from Princess Anne, on property donated by Samuel Wilson.

Tuition was five thousand pounds, a fortune considering the average cost of a new building in Princess Anne at the time, including land purchase, was less than eight hundred pounds. However, this school offered amenities Somerset's private schoolhouse did not. In addition to living arrangements for all students, Somerset Academy provided education in the arts and sciences, far beyond the reading and writing skills taught at the aging 1726 school on the Manokin River.

For nearly a quarter of a century, wealthy students from Somerset, Worcester and Dorchester Counties in Maryland; Accomack and Northampton Counties in Virginia and Sussex County in Delaware attended school at the academy. Their studies there came to an end when the academy burned in 1797, possibly at the hands of an arsonist.

Meanwhile, local students attending the free school on the Manokin River in 1771 moved into a new building on the Wicomico River. Named in honor of presiding Maryland governor Robert Eden, it remained in use until 1796, when it was declared unhealthy and sold by the General Assembly. Unhealthy or not, the Eden building resumed its duties as a school from 1797 to 1802 when trustees of Somerset Academy rented it for use until a new permanent academy building could be constructed.

Construction was taking place in areas outside Princess Anne, as well. Around 1733, Thomas Williams built a home on property, near Gales Creek in Kingston, that he inherited from William Planner Jr. Today that property is known as Williams Green, or Williams Conquest.

Five years later, the Reverend Alexander Adams settled the 320-acre plantation Brentwood near Allen on property originally patented in 1667 as Smith's Adventure. Becoming the director of Stepney Parish in 1704, he served as its rector until his death in 1769. Records show Adams owned twenty slaves, who resided in quarters on the plantation. The land also featured two barns, a sawmill and a milk house.

Another early eighteenth-century home, Glanville's Lot, was built on a five-hundred-acre parcel originally surveyed for William Glanville on March 11, 1663, on the Manokin River. Captain John Tunstall operated a shipyard on the lot in the 1740s, when it was resurveyed for the Reverend James Robinson.

The Reward, yet another grand plantation house, was constructed at Williams Point in 1750 by Stephen White, who inherited the land from Colonel Stevens. Between 1759 and 1772, White's grandson, Elias, who had received the 626-acre plantation in a family will, mortgaged and sold large portions of the land. David Williams purchased the remaining 488 acres, then called White's Gift, on November 22, 1773, for 1,065 pounds.

Around the same time the Reward was built, construction began anew at John Elzey's former thousand-acre estate, Almodington, near modern-day Oriole. In 1667, Elzey's son, Arnold, took over Almodington, leaving the estate to his own children, John, Sarah and Elizabeth. While Arnold's daughters received the riverfront house on the plantation, John inherited the bulk of the property and set out to build his own house. That house, which still stands today under the original plantation's name, was constructed circa 1750.

Arlington, near today's town of Westover, was yet another plantation house built around this time on property dubbed Wilson's Lot, inherited from Ephraim Wilson upon the death of his father, David. By 1791, the lot also contained a barn, a corn house and slave quarters.

Three more homes constructed near Princess Anne in the mid-eighteenth century still stand today. Likely built between 1754 and 1760, the Waddy house was constructed on a plantation known as Killmonum, near the head of the Manokin River and purchased from James and William Gray by Jarvis Ballard. Killmonum was made by combining three former plantations—Derry, Goldsmith's Delight and Smith's Resolve—in the early 1700s.

The second, Harrington, was built after 1741 by Thomas Holbrook on a plantation of nearly 1,000 acres east of the Wicomico River near the area known today as Mount Vernon. By the end of the eighteenth century, the plantation had become a tenant farm, overseen by Samuel Covington. The third, Cherry Grove, was constructed by Thomas

Jones on the 370-acre Bridger's Lot plantation, patented in 1748. Jones passed the home on to his son, William, upon his death in 1766.

Several other notable homes were built throughout the county from about 1750 to the early 1760s. One was Westover—the mansion, not the town—built by Samuel Wilson on Back Creek on a large plantation formed by combining the former Great Hopes and Dear Purchase plantations near the modern-day town of Westover. In a nod to history, the municipal golf course in the town of Westover was named in honor of the original Great Hopes plantation when the course was dedicated in 1995.

Another was Hayward's Lot, on land surveyed for Thomas Hayward in 1734. This 740-acre plantation was made up of portions from the former Williams Hope and Blake's Hope plantations near modern-day Pocomoke City. A clerk of the Somerset County Court, Hayward died in 1751, leaving the land to his son, Thomas Jr. The younger Hayward married into the Elzeys, of Almodington fame, two years later when he wed Sarah Elzey. The brick plantation house, still standing on this property, likely was built just before or during the early years of their marriage.

One of the most well known houses built during this era was the ornate Waterloo, constructed near Princess Anne in the early 1750s. Its builder, Henry Waggaman, was a prominent member of Somerset society, serving as an elder of the Manokin Presbyterian Church as well as one of the county's representatives at the General Assembly from 1750 to 1760. The estate on which Waterloo was built was nearly as old as Somerset County, patented to Richard Carey on November 20, 1666, as "Carey's Purchase." Waggaman bought the property as part of a series of land investments throughout the county. By the time the Waggaman family sold the bulk of Carey's Purchase in 1803, the estate had grown to more than 1,700 acres.

Around 1767, the home Windsor was built on a farm owned by Isaac Costen on a tract of land later known as the Burton Cannon Farm, near Cokesbury. Another home that still stands, the Bannister house, was built by Charles Bannister in 1770 on a 160-acre tract south of the Manokin River in what is today Revells Neck. Part of another historic home, the Gunby-Lankford house, is believed to have been built during this period as well, in what is now the Cash Corner neighborhood just outside Crisfield.

In addition to homesteads, small communities also began to crop up, especially along the Little Annemessex River and Pocomoke Sound. They included Somers Cove, Cork, Ape's Hole, Rumbling Point, Quindocqua, Tulls Corner and Jenkins Creek.

For all the growth, construction and optimism found throughout the county during this time, political tensions elsewhere were rising. While the American colonists still saw themselves as loyalists to the British throne, English leaders began to calculate new ways to profit from their holdings in the Americas.

The notion was not entirely selfish. King George III was seeking ways to pay off the debts incurred while fighting the French for North American territories during the Seven Years' War. The war added greatly to the British Empire, capturing the New France area of Canada, Spanish Florida and Native American territories east of the Mississippi River.

While British taxation in the colonies was not a new concept, the enforcement of taxation laws was. As enforcement tightened, colonists began to bristle. A new tax on sugar in 1764, coupled with passage of a British law, the Currency Act, that devalued colonial scrip and barred colonies from issuing more, caused even greater tension. The next year, the Stamp Act was passed, requiring a British tax stamp to be affixed to all printed materials distributed in the colonies. Funds accumulated through stamp purchases went directly into the British coffers.

The slogan "no taxation without representation" spread throughout the seaboard, marking the beginning of a unity seldom before seen among the thirteen original colonies. Under the movement, colonists pushed for laws that would allow only their individual colonial governments, not the British kingdom—where they no longer had a voice in Parliament—to levy taxes upon them. They also began to boycott most goods imported from England, especially after the Townshend Acts of 1767 further taxed imports to colonial ports.

Sensing a growing hostility in the colonies, British officials had already taken measures to keep them from expanding beyond their current boundaries. The Proclamation of 1763 barred expansion over the Appalachian Mountains, though it was not successful and was later amended to allow growth in those areas. More successful was the Quebec Act of 1774, which extended the southern boundary of New France to the Ohio River, effectively shutting out colonists' claims to land in that area.

By then, colonial dissent had become much more apparent. In 1768, the British seized the freight ship *Liberty*, captained by John Hancock, charging him with smuggling tea into the colonies, untaxed. Though the charges eventually were dropped, smuggling was indeed a problem for the British-owned East India Company, which depended in part on sales in the colonies.

Angered by his arrest, Hancock organized a boycott of East India tea throughout the colonies. Sales plummeted from 320,000 pounds in 1768 to a scant 520 pounds in 1773. That year, Parliament passed the Tea Act, allowing the East India Company to sell tea directly to the colonies without paying taxes. While this allowed East India to sell tea at prices lower than smugglers, it raised the colonists' ire even more. Tea smuggling had become quite a profitable livelihood for some, and the Tea Act cut taxes only for East India, not the colonists.

The Sons of Liberty, an underground organization formed to instigate the colonies' secession from England, called for protests in New York, Philadelphia and Boston. The latter protest went down in history as the Boston Tea Party, during which Sons of Liberty members, disguised as Native Americans, boarded East India ships in Boston Harbor and dumped forty-five tons of tea overboard. The total loss was estimated at ten thousand pounds.

The British government responded not only by demanding repayment for the tea, but by closing the port of Boston as part of the four acts, deemed the Intolerable Acts, that led to the Revolutionary War. Three of the acts, including the one that closed Boston Harbor, were aimed directly at removing power from the Massachusetts government. The fourth, however, hindered all thirteen colonies by mandating private citizens to house British troops in their homes if requested.

If local stories are true, some Marylanders responded to the Intolerable Acts by emulating their colonial brethren in Boston. The residents of Chestertown, in what is now Kent County, met in May 1774 and made a decision to boycott tea altogether. These same residents are said by some to have then gathered at the center of town and marched to the Chester River, where the ship *Geddes* carried a cargo of tea. The protestors allegedly dumped that cargo into the river in support of the Sons of Liberty.

No evidence beyond personal remembrances, passed down through generations, exists to corroborate that event. However, in the twenty-first century, the citizens of Chestertown still gather for a reenactment of the event each May.

If the people of Somerset County were that passionate about the events taking place in England, the records do not show it. If anything, there exists more evidence that many residents in Somerset remained fiercely loyal to the British kingdom. However, they, like all other colonists, were about to become involved in the war that would create a new country—the United States of America.

Chapter 4

Fighting for Independence

While Northern colonies were largely in favor of waging a war for independence against the British, support never swelled in Somerset County. In southern Somerset especially, colonists were still loyal to the crown.

Fighting remained largely away from the Eastern Shore, disinteresting many of its residents. In fact, for the first three years of the war, from 1775 to 1778, many Eastern Shore militias were encouraged to remain on active duty rather than join others in the Northern colonies.

Still, there were a handful of soldiers from Somerset known to have fought alongside other colonists in the Revolutionary War during those early years, sixty-three in all, including Levin Boston, Henry Miles, Travers Sterling, Ephraim Sterling, Henry Sterling, Thomas Nelson, Joshua Tull, John Turpin and William Whittington. Two others, Jonathan and William Sterling, both of the Annemessex area, fought on behalf of the British.

Perhaps the best-known Revolutionary War soldier from Somerset County was General John Gale. The only Somerset general from the war was born September 15, 1753, on his family's plantation on the Gale Creek, between what is today Kingston and Marion Station. Joining the Colonial Army as a second lieutenant on December 20, 1776, he was taken prisoner at Staten Island, New York, in August 1777. He continued to serve throughout the war until 1783, rising to his retiring rank of general. He died March 3, 1812, and was buried at his family's plantation.

Somerset residents held important positions off the battlefield, as well. When the time came to sign the Declaration of Independence on July 4, 1776, one of those ratifying the document was a Somerset County native. Born in Princess Anne in 1741, Samuel Chase was elected as a Maryland representative to the Continental Congress in 1774 and re-elected in 1775, serving until 1778.

A lawyer, Chase spent most of his professional life not in Somerset County, but in Annapolis, then Baltimore, where he was later appointed chief justice of the Court of Maryland. In 1796 he was appointed as a justice of the Supreme Court of the United States. He remained in that position until his death on June 19, 1811.

While the colonists had their independence on paper in 1776, it was clearly no reflection on what the next seven years would bring. As the war continued, it began having more impact on Somerset, if somewhat indirectly.

Though there has been talk of pirates—including the infamous Blackbeard—plundering Somerset villages, little proof exists that the types of pirates that inhabited the area bore any resemblance to those found in the Caribbean during the eighteenth and nineteenth centuries. However, pirates did exist in Somerset County in the form of British loyalists seeking supplies for troops and monetary gain for themselves.

One such pirate was Joseph Wheland Jr., who terrorized the Chesapeake region throughout much of the Revolution. While carrying goods from Somerset County through the Potomac River in early 1776, he sought to trade with a British fleet led by John Murray, Lord Dunmore, royal governor of Virginia. By that June, under Lord Dunmore's influence, Wheland had become a full-fledged commander of a squadron of loyalists set on raiding the Eastern Shore.

Wheland's squadron included a pilot boat, an armed schooner and two ten-gun sloops. After carrying out his first raid on Hopkins Island, in Dorchester County, he set his sights on Somerset. One of his first actions there was to seek revenge on a wealthy plantation owner named William Roberts in what is today Dame's Quarter. Roberts, it seems, was an enemy of one of Wheland's crewmen, and enemies had to be dealt with.

Under cover of darkness, the crew kidnapped Roberts from his bed, bound him and robbed him of both slaves and material goods before carrying him off as a prisoner. So abundant was loyalist pirate, or "picaroon," activity in this area that it earned the name Damned Quarter and another nearby community Devil's Island. In the 1800s, as an appeal to Christian sensitivities, these areas were renamed Dames Quarter and Deal Island. Rogues Point on Smith Island suffered the same fate with a name change to Rhodes Point.

An interesting note is the intrinsic value picaroons and the Royal Navy saw in slaves, which often were taken during raids such as the one against Roberts. In the Northern colonies, freed slaves often fought alongside Caucasians in militias. On the Eastern Shore and points south, however, most slaves were not given the freedom to fight on behalf of the Continental cause.

Slaves captured by the picaroons not only helped deplete the economy of the Eastern Shore, which depended on them for virtually free labor, but added to the British cause, where they often were offered freedom in exchange for joining the royal forces. In fact, the British used this promise as a recruiting tool. In all, between seventy-five thousand and one hundred thousand runaway slaves from the colonies are estimated to have joined the British military. Some strategists figured the threat of lost slaves alone would be enough to cause colonists to encourage their leaders to end the war and accept British rule.

The picaroons, under Wheland's command, struck again shortly after the Roberts attack, burning the home of another enemy, Samuel McChester, at Nanticoke Point. Residents of areas that still clung fiercely to British loyalties, including Perryhawkin and Marumsco, actually cheered their efforts. These pirates had no method or strategy in their attacks but to plunder. This confounded the Somerset County militia, whose leaders called for assistance from all surrounding counties. By the time those militias responded, however, it was too late. Wheland had moved on, for the time being, anyway.

Another notorious picaroon based in Somerset County was Captain Roache. He first appears in the records in connection with an act of piracy committed March 30, 1779, against a schooner off the coast of Damned Quarter. Four men reportedly boarded the boat, seizing ten gallons of brandy, a keg and a bag of corn while holding the two-man crew at gunpoint. The incident almost turned deadly when one of the picaroons discovered a Continental flag onboard; however, the crew was given a reprieve after swearing loyalty to England.

Upon learning of the event, Colonel George Dashiell of Somerset County sent a message to Governor Thomas Johnson, requesting permission to use militia force against picaroons in the future. He also asked for several armed ships to help expedite the cause.

Still more picaroons emerged. Stephen Mister, once a crewmember with Wheland, struck out on his own in 1779, operating an armed barge from his base on the Annemessex River. His exploits took him from the mouth of the Nanticoke River into Tangier Sound, where he not only plundered plantations, but shanghaied boats for use by the British. These boats reportedly were dispatched to Smith Island, where Mister's uncle, Marmaduke, would hold them until British soldiers arrived. Popular legend says Marmaduke Mister was rewarded for his services in picaroon treasure, and that treasure is still buried at Kizzie's Point.

That April, the Maryland navy dispatched two schooners, *Dolphin* and *Plater*, to Tangier Sound with the expressed purpose of finding Stephen Mister and another picaroon, Smith Carmine. Joined by the Somerset and Dorchester County militias, their efforts were in vain. When it was believed the two pirates had traveled up the Pocomoke River, its entrance was sealed off with the hope of capturing Mister and Carmine. The Maryland officers also blockaded Tangier Sound in hopes of keeping Mister away from any contacts he may have had on Smith Island.

Without success, the schooners were dispatched on another mission. However, the militias did not give up hope. Their members began searching all boats sailing through Hooper's Strait in Dorchester County. When that did not work, Colonel Dashiell surmised Mister may have traveled to his father's home on the Honga River. With the heightened presence of British soldiers in the area, officials feared the picaroons might have joined the British navy as a means of escape.

Whether that was Carmine's fate is unknown. However, Mister eventually was captured—not in Maryland, but in Virginia, as he continued his pirate ways through August 1780.

By September 1779, the picaroon problem had gotten out of control. By the end of that month, residents in the Dorchester County town of Vienna, bordering Somerset County to the north, had petitioned Governor Johnson for six cannons to help defend the area. Vienna itself housed several Continental ships. However, by the time the governor responded, it was too late.

The picaroons and members of the British fleet burned the Continental ships at Vienna and after plundering the town, set their sights on Somerset and Worcester Counties. On September 29, Colonel Joseph Dashiell of Snow Hill delivered a report to the governor that the picaroons and British soldiers had raided riverside villages along twenty miles of the two lower shore counties. They burned a Continental ship belonging to Maryland navy Captain Robert Dashiell and cleaned out the homes and stores of many civilians. Another Continental officer, Colonel John Henry, was said to have suffered a loss of thirty thousand pounds in goods and damages.

Ships loaded with corn and pork for the Continental army were also captured. Because so many local residents were involved in the large-scale attack, many militia members refused to fight. The raiders returned to their base in Damned Quarter richer and happy to have helped the British cause.

By 1780, picaroon sightings in Somerset County were at an all-time high. One crafty pirate of this time was John Botsworth, a former ship's carpenter from Annapolis who captained picaroon ships on the Annemessex. While his crew faced off against one patriot ship, he cast himself in chains so in the event of capture, he could claim he had been fighting with the picaroons against his will.

That same year, Wheland reappeared on the scene. Having previously been arrested, he was released after more than four years when Somerset residents Samuel Covington and Thomas Holbrook posted ten thousand pounds of bail on his behalf in Baltimore. Wheland claimed to have disavowed loyalty to the British, but the truth soon emerged. Captains of vessels captured once again named Wheland as the culprit. On December 11, 1780, the pirate neglected to show for his hearing before Governor Thomas Lee to answer to charges of high treason, indebting Covington and Holbrook for the full ten-thousand-pound bond.

Soon, Wheland rebuilt his crew, this time maintaining a smaller number of lieutenants who acted more as co-captains than subordinates. They included Shadrack Horseman, Michael Timmons and William Timmons Jr. of Hooper's Strait. They commanded their own militia of four armed barges, often sailing with or near similar barges under the British flag. Wheland developed a code of recognition for these barges: raising and lowering the mainsail three times, then hoisting a Union Jack.

With piracy in the area at its worst since the war began, Colonel Joseph Dashiell petitioned the governor, as Colonel George Dashiell had done the year before, for permission to use militia force to apprehend picaroons, specifically Wheland, whom he believed could be tracked in Somerset County. However, he also wanted to take the initiative a step further, ridding the islands in the Chesapeake Bay of all occupants to ensure no British or picaroon threat existed on those islands.

By 1781, the Maryland navy existed in name only. Nearly all of its ships had been destroyed or auctioned off to help pay other expenses of Maryland's participation in the war. On March 21, twenty-six residents of Somerset County, led by Captain Zedekiah Whaley, proposed to the General Assembly the construction of a fifty-foot barge with room for a sixty-man crew and a twenty-four-pound bow gun for use as protection against picaroons in the county.

While the proposed budget for the vessel was less than 150 pounds, the Maryland treasury was completely empty. When the assembly denied the citizens' request, they banded together and raised the money themselves, building the barge *Protector* at a shipyard in Snow Hill.

Bold as they were, even the picaroons knew enough to run from a twenty-four-pound gun. *Protector* sailed with great success, driving the pirates from the Pocomoke region, if not from Damned Quarter. This success inspired other Eastern Shore colonists. Queen Anne's and Talbot Counties banded together to build their own armed barge, *Experiment*, followed by Dorchester County with the barge *Defence*.

With this small navy in place, the colonists were able to capture British and picaroon barges to add to the fleet. Finally, that July, Maryland officials resurrected the Maryland navy with its own flotilla of barges. The picaroon raids continued, but at least now the people of Somerset and surrounding counties had some measure of defense.

In early 1777, some four hundred British supporters in Somerset and Worcester Counties tried to stage an uprising against the Continentals. This movement failed only because expected help from British troops never arrived. As a result, two thousand militia troops were ordered stationed on the Eastern Shore to help ensure such an event did not happen again. Even then, however, there were more British supporters than patriots.

The picaroon attacks had changed that. Because the pirates were, in effect, helping the British, the Royal Navy offered no protection against them. At the same time, the picaroons were disrupting trade among nearly all Eastern Shore merchants, Continental and British, and costing them thousands of pounds in looting and damage. By the early 1780s, most of the Eastern Shore, Somerset County included, was as pro-Continental as the Northern colonies.

On July 31, 1772, Zedekiah Whaley, who had been named commodore of the Maryland navy earlier that year, received orders to join forces with French armed vessels on the York River. During Whaley's absence, a call for help again rang out from Colonel Joseph Dashiell. Picaroons were again looting Worcester County.

Whaley and his three barges—Somerset's *Protector*, which he manned himself; Dorchester's *Defence*, captained by Solomon Frazier; and a third, *Terrible*, captained by Robert Dashiell—sailed into Baltimore from the York in September without ever having found the French vessels. However, he did bring with him four picaroon boats captured during the voyage. Almost immediately, he was dispatched again in a further campaign against the picaroons. This time, he was joined by the barge *Fearnaught*, captained by Levin Speeden, and the armed supply tender *Flying Fish*, captained by Daniel Bryan.

Stationed near Cape Charles, Whaley received word that several small boats, either picaroon or British in nature, were causing damage at Janes Island in lower Somerset. He removed his fleet to a new base in Onancock Creek to more easily monitor activity in Tangier Sound. On November 12, Whaley received word that five picaroon barges had been spotted off the Delmarva Peninsula. He suspected they planned to land at Gwynn's Island, Virginia.

Indeed the picaroons did anchor there, but fled as soon as they saw Whaley's men coming. Frazier, in *Defence*, caught one of the picaroon barges, *Jolly Tar*, nabbing at least nine pirates in the process. Chasing the remaining barges to the mouth of the Chesapeake, Whaley found two more picaroon ships anchored at Smith Island, Virginia. They, too, fled. Whaley did not let up the chase until the picaroons were safely in Atlantic waters, far away from their intended targets on the Eastern Shore—or so he thought.

As Whaley led his barges back to the Pocomoke River, the picaroons returned to the area, meeting in Chincoteague, Virginia. Upon sailing back to Onancock Creek several days later with the intention of resuming vigilance of Tangier Sound, Whaley and his crew spied the picaroon fleet once again, this time joined by another ship. They were sailing for Captain Smith's original Russell Isles, by now renamed the Tangier Islands.

Because Whaley's fleet was outnumbered—a total of six picaroon barges plus the seventh ship had now taken up the fray—he sent word on Colonel John Cropper of Accomack County, Virginia, asking for assistance. Cropper sent two small barges: *Victory*, a former picaroon ship, and *Langodoc*. Meanwhile, Frazier sailed into Tangier Island, Virginia, to gain more information on the picaroon fleet. Disguised as a British loyalist, right down to flying a Union Jack from *Defence*, he learned that supporters there had no idea Whaley's men were lying in wait between Watts Island and Onancock.

Later that night, in anticipation of catching the picaroon fleet by surprise, Whaley and his barges anchored off Fox Island. It became clear that *Victory* could not keep up, and that barge was dispatched back to Virginia. Hoping for another leg up on the picaroons, Whaley sent his lieutenant, Samuel Handy, who was piloting *Langodoc*, ashore on Fox Island to determine whether the pirates had stopped there. Indeed they had, Handy learned, and they were headed toward Kedges Strait.

Whaley and his men followed their path, anchoring off Janes Island about four o'clock in the morning of November 30. By six o'clock, the picaroon fleet was spotted, and a chase began. By nine o'clock, with both flotillas less than a mile apart, battle began. Two of the picaroon ships fired first upon *Defence*, and Frazier shot back. Those were the first shots of the Battle of the Barges, fought entirely in Somerset County and said to have been among the bloodiest naval battles of the Revolutionary War.

Fearnaught was the next Maryland barge to fire, its six-pound gun blowing to pieces with its first shot. *Protector* surged to the forefront, taking on the entire picaroon fleet with its eighteen-pound gun. *Fearnaught* served as backup with two twelve-pound guns, two four-pound guns, a swivel gun and individual muskets. The picaroons were down—until *Protector* got a little too close.

Moving within fifty yards of the picaroon fleet, Whaley found himself the immediate target of all six enemy barges. A cartridge meant for one of *Protector*'s guns broke, spilling powder all over the deck. A flash from a second of the ship's guns ignited it, burning several crewmembers. Two picaroon ships moved closer to board *Protector* as the rest turned their fire on *Defence*. *Flying Fish*, *Terrible* and *Langodoc* had already retreated. Seeing two picaroon ships trying to board *Defence*, Speeden and *Fearnaught* also retreated, though Speeden did fire one final twelve-pound round at the picaroons before leaving their range.

Now badly outnumbered, Frazier also called retreat. *Flying Fish* and *Langodoc* sailed for shelter in the Annemessex River. The picaroons left them alone, instead going after *Defence* and *Fearnaught*. They finally gave up the chase around four o'clock in the afternoon as the Maryland ships reached the upper entrance to Hooper's Strait.

Colonel Cropper of Accomack County later offered an eyewitness account in a letter to Maryland Governor William Paca, calling the battle "a continual shower of musket bullets, pikes, cold shot, cutlasses and iron stantials." In all, the battle lasted less than thirty minutes.

For all the large guns trained on his boat, Whaley was killed by a simple musket shot. Most crew aboard *Protector* still alive at the time of his death allegedly were thrown overboard or killed once the picaroons boarded. Of the sixty-five colonists engaged in the battle, twenty-five died and twenty-nine were wounded.

Cropper, captured during the battle, negotiated freedom for himself and his men in exchange for taking the wounded picaroons ashore and making sure they received proper treatment. He made the deal with John Kidd, a Virginia loyalist who claimed to lead the enemy fleet. In reality, it was Joseph Wheland who had masterminded the battle. With Whaley out of the way, he would continue plundering until the Treaty of Paris was signed, ending the war the next year.

In Annapolis, Paca was distraught over news of the battle. Cropper charged that all men but Whaley and his crew were cowards. Upon appearing before the governor, Frazier and Speeden requested an inquiry and were reinstated after being held harmless in the incident. Zadock Botfield, the lieutenant of *Fearnaught*, was suspended, but reinstated after just two days. Robert Dashiell was ultimately discharged from the Maryland navy.

The Treaty of Paris signaled better times on the Eastern Shore, now a part of the officially recognized United States of America. The home-building boom that had tapered off at the beginning of the revolution recommenced, giving the area some of its most ornate dwellings. Chief among them were Beverly and Teackle Mansions, which remain showplaces of Somerset County today.

Somerset's wealthiest landowner of the day, Nehemiah King II, built Beverly between 1785 and 1796 near Princess Anne. With an estimated twenty thousand dollars in holdings, King was undisputedly the richest man in the region. In addition to the main house, his plantation included a barn, granary, stable, smokehouse, milk house, lumber house, meat house, schoolhouse, poultry house, icehouse, blacksmith shop and windmill, several other storage buildings and an orchard featuring about 850 apple and peach trees.

For many years, however, Beverly's most notable feature has been the rumor that a room once existed under its main stairwell to provide shelter to Napoleon Bonaparte following a planned escape from St. Helena Island, where he was exiled in 1815. That rumor remains unsubstantiated.

Teackle Mansion, built about 1802 by Dennis Littleton Teackle, was the focal point of his nine-acre plantation, Teackletonia. Its size and the amount of detail put into the building indicate how prominent Teackle was. A merchant dealing largely in lumber, under the trade name Teackle and Company, Teackle was one of the richest people in Somerset County at this time. In 1805, he reportedly even supplied lumber for construction of the U.S. Capitol.

However, much of his money came from importing and exporting goods in England and the Caribbean. He owned a trade ship, *Philanthropist*, able to send goods from the colonies, like corn and lumber, to the Bahamas in exchange for coffee, cocoa and sugar,

Teackle Mansion, built about 1802 by Dennis Littleton Teackle, was the focal point of his nine-acre plantation, Teackletonia, in Princess Anne. In the early twenty-first century, Teackle Mansion remains one of the county's most prominent structures.

all of which fetched top prices in ports like Baltimore. He even contracted with the U.S. Navy to supply lumber for its earliest fleet.

Despite this prosperity, he was met twice with devastating financial loss. In 1807, he was forced to sell the mansion to pay creditors. He repurchased it in 1815, only to be forced to sell it again in 1839. In 1816, he also purchased land in Barren Creek, now Mardela Springs in Wicomico County, with the idea of turning it into a health resort featuring local mineral water.

In Somerset County, he was president of the Bank of Somerset and brought the idea of steam power to the Eastern Shore with his steam mill, built on the Manokin River in 1815. He was elected as a Somerset representative to the Maryland House of Delegates in 1824, serving until 1836. He also served as a spokesman to the U.S. Congress.

For all his one-time wealth, Teackle died—with just twenty-five dollars to his name—while on business in Baltimore. His ornate mansion, a symbol of Somerset County now for more than two centuries, went on to national fame as the setting for the 1884 George Alfred Townsend book *The Entailed Hat*, telling the story of another famous Eastern Shore (but not Somerset County) resident, Patty Cannon.

Schools and churches also came into play again following the Revolution. Somerset Academy, burned in 1797, was rebuilt and reopened November 23, 1802. An early handbook offers some of the rules of the time:

The hours of study in Summer are from 6 to 8 and from sunrise to 8 in Winter, and from 9 to 12, 2 to 5 and 7 to 9 all the school year.

No student is supposed to wander from his room after 8 o'clock in the evening.

No student shall be suffered to carry victuals with him from the dining room, nor to eat in his room.

No student shall enter the town of Princess Anne without special permission of his tutor, his parents, or guardian.

The forenoon of every Saturday shall be spent in learning and pronouncing English, one-half of the boys writing letters and composing on some Theme, and the other pronouncing pieces and so alternating.

There shall be a general examination every quarter, those in the Spring and Fall to be attended by the board, and open to all friends of literature. The examination in the Spring to commence of the first Wednesday in May, and in the fall on the Wednesday proceeding the last Tuesday of August.

After the examinations in the Spring there shall be a vacation of three weeks, and after the examinations in the fall a vacation of five weeks.

The students shall attend prayers at the opening and close of each day, and shall behave themselves in a decent and reverent manner during that time. They shall likewise attend public worship on the Sabbath Day when opportunity offers, the choice of place left to themselves. They shall endeavor to sanctify the Sabbath Day by refraining from amusement, labor or study. Every student shall keep a Bible or Testament in his room, a part of which the Principal may require him to read on the Sabbath Day with a view to his being examined on the contents in the evening.

Even the daily menu was spelled out in advance. At all meals, students were served coffee, tea, hot chocolate or milk, and cornbread with butter or wheat biscuits without butter. The choice was the principal's, not the students'. Dinners consisted of bacon four times each week with fresh provisions twice a week from March 1 through the August vacation. Meals after the August vacation consisted of bacon twice a week and pork, beef or mutton four times a week. The seventh dinner of the week was always declared a "Bunyan Day," during which no meat was served. So went education in Somerset County for the next ninety years.

The same decade the new Somerset Academy was dedicated, residents at the county's southern end also were bracing for change—in a good way. In 1810, the Reverend Thomas Carron officially organized Asbury Methodist Church in Lawsonia. While the first service was held in the home of Hance Lawson, near today's Jenkins Creek

Bridge, a formal church building was constructed before the year's end. Located at the intersection of what are now Lawsonia and Boone Roads, the building remained the church's home until 1847, when a larger structure was built to house the congregation near the church's current location on Lawsonia Road at Asbury Avenue.

Methodism in Somerset County—indeed, throughout the Eastern Shore—marked a vast change in the religious thinking of the area after the revolution. The first home of this religion in lower Somerset was the Miles Meeting House, built in 1784 on a tract of land in Hopewell purchased from Benjamin and Betsy Williams. Its name changed to St. Peter's Methodist Church in 1813.

It was at a camp meeting at this church that Joshua Thomas, the famed "Parson of the Islands" was converted in 1807. Born in Potato Neck (now known as Fairmount) on August 30, 1776, Thomas moved from Somerset County very early in life. His father, John, died of a dog bite while visiting relatives in Tangier Island, Virginia, while Joshua was only a child. Following this, Joshua's mother, Martha, moved the family to Tangier, where she remarried. Prayer was very important in the Thomas household, for good fishing skills bequeathed by the Lord were the only thing that stood between the Thomases and hunger.

As a young man, following the death of his mother, Thomas lived and apprenticed with fisherman David Tyler on Smith Island. Through Tyler, he honed his boating skills and, perhaps more importantly, learned about Methodism. Prayer served the young Thomas once again during this time when he prayed to find a good wife. He found two. Thomas married Rachel Evans, daughter of Richard and Molly Crockett Evans, on September 10, 1797, at age twenty-three. Upon her death, he remarried to Charlotte Bradshaw, daughter of Richard and Arabella Mister Bradshaw, on September 30, 1914.

Because no full-time preacher existed on Smith Island, the Reverend Joshua Reese, rector of Stepney Parish from 1799 to 1801, sometimes was asked to sail over from the mainland and offer a guest sermon. Because of his boating and canoeing skills, Thomas often was asked to provide the preacher's transportation. This helped spark an interest in religion, and he soon began attending services regularly at the chapel near the head of Coulbourn Creek, forerunner to St. Paul's Church at Quindocqua.

One Sunday when Thomas reached the church, he learned the Reverend Reese was away. A man by the name of William Miles invited Thomas to attend St. Peter's. Reluctantly, he went. It was here the future preacher would eventually give his first sermon. Following his conversion to Methodism, Thomas became a circuit preacher. Aboard his boat, *Methodist*, he ministered throughout Somerset County, but became most famous for his fiery sermons in underserved areas including Deal, Smith and Tangier Islands. Even the British lined up to listen at one point.

During the War of 1812, the Royal Navy made Tangier Sound its base of operations during maneuvers in the Chesapeake Bay. Living on Tangier Island, Virginia, at the time, Thomas appealed to the soldier's Christian sensibilities, persuading them to quarter in an empty building instead of taking one from an existing occupant by force. He also successfully requested that they spare the trees surrounding the island's Methodist campground.

More than a century and a half following Joshua Thomas's death, the religious camp meetings for which he was famous remain a Somerset tradition. Among the most popular is the one held annually on Smith Island, seen here circa 1910.

However, the sermon that made him a legend came when the British set out to attack Baltimore in 1814. Asking the admiral to gather his troops for a sermon prior to leaving Tangier Sound, Thomas stood before about twelve thousand British soldiers and warned them God would not look favorably upon their run at Baltimore. Indeed, their historic attack on Fort McHenry failed.

The War of 1812 marked a unique time in Somerset history, for it was the first time a Somerset man helmed the state. Born September 4, 1757, near Monie, Levin Winder joined the Continental army during the Revolutionary War, advancing to the rank of lieutenant colonel by the time of his discharge. A staunch Federalist, he was appointed a major general of the militia by Governor Thomas Lee in 1794. Winder was elected as a Somerset representative to the Maryland House of Delegates in 1806, becoming the House Speaker two years later.

Elected as Maryland's governor on November 23, 1812, as an anti-war advocate, he requested help from the federal government to ward off British attacks. When that failed, he sent out an impassioned plea to the citizens of Maryland to defend the state. His efforts were instrumental to the victory at Fort McHenry.

Before leaving office in 1816, Winder performed one more act, perhaps earning him more fame in Maryland than he received as the governor who saw the state through the War of 1812. On July 4, 1815, he laid the cornerstone for the Washington Monument in

Elected Maryland's governor on November 23, 1812, as an anti-war advocate, Levin Winder sent out an impassioned plea to the citizens of Maryland to defend the state against the British. His efforts were instrumental to the victory at Fort McHenry.

Baltimore as grand master of the Ancient Free and Accepted Masons of Maryland. He passed away on July 1, 1819, just three years after stepping down from governorship.

At least three Somerset County residents—John Coulbourn, William Milbourne and McKenna Tawes, all of the Annamessex area—are on the books as having heeded the call to fight. While the Fort McHenry battle became the war's most famous, there were plenty of other skirmishes throughout. One smaller fight occurred just outside Annemessex. Much as the picaroons did during the Revolutionary War, British soldiers held no qualms about raiding homesteads and villages for supplies. While British troops were encamped on Joshua Thomas's Tangier Island, one island resident sailed a skiff to the mainland one night to warn them of an impending raid.

When the soldiers arrived the next morning in small, open boats, much of the male population of Annemessex was waiting for them on the shore, using their wagons to form a barricade and firing with all the muskets available to them in what would be called the Battle of Jenkins Creek. Without the benefit of cover or much weaponry—their big ships were anchored farther away from shore—the British finally retreated after about three hours.

One interesting note: following the War of 1812, the U.S. Navy surveyed Tangier Island as the site of a possible naval base to help protect Tangier Sound against future foreign occupation. The base never materialized.

By 1815, Somerset County had survived two wars in four decades, becoming part of a new nation in the process. Little did its residents know they had only another half century before that nation itself fell apart.

Chapter 5

Somerset and the Civil War

Truly independent for the first time, the people of Somerset County spent much of the time between 1815 and 1850 building the area into one many today would find recognizable. In Princess Anne, an 1820 fire at the courthouse led to the establishment of a new court building at the corner of Prince William and Bridge Streets.

Most of the county's public records, which were saved from the fire, were stored in the vault of a bank, owned by Dennis Littleton Teackle on that site, until the new courthouse replaced it. Like the structure that came before it, this new courthouse was used not only for legal services, but for recreation and church gatherings, as well. In fact, the Continental Band of Somerset often used the jury room for rehearsals in the 1860s.

The county saw its first newspaper in April 1827, when the Princess Anne-based *Village Herald* began publication. Several others followed, including the *Somerset Iris and Messenger of Truth* in 1828, *People's Press* in 1836, *Somerset Union* in 1856 and *Somerset Herald* in 1861.

Some areas of Somerset even had their own currency, as was fairly common among American settlements at the time. Banknotes produced by the Bank of Somerset spent well during the early 1800s. During the Civil War years, a series of Somerset-Worcester banknotes were produced for regional trade on the lower Eastern Shore. No matter if the Union or the Confederacy won, these notes would still be bankable.

Meanwhile, Methodism continued to spread throughout the county and indeed the Eastern Shore as a whole. Congregations sprung up in modern-day Oriole in 1810, Princess Anne in 1817, Quindocqua in 1820, Rehobeth in 1830 and Fairmount in 1842. In 1828, Joshua Thomas founded an annual Methodist camp meeting in Deal Island at Old Hill, on a site no longer in existence due to more than a century of erosion. In 1850, a new church in Deal Island, at Parks Grove, was built as Joshua Thomas Chapel. This was the church in which the famed parson reportedly delivered his final sermon. Passing away three years following the chapel's construction, he was buried there in 1853.

Somers Cove, in lower Somerset County, saw its first "church" about 1860. Nicknamed "the Ark," the church actually was a canal barge floated at high tide onto the mudflats at the edge of the village. While its chief use was as an oyster house, possibly the first one in this area, its owner, a Mr. Denike, conducted church and Sunday school services aboard the dry-docked vessel every Sunday.

During the Civil War years, a series of Somerset-Worcester banknotes were produced for regional trade on the lower Eastern Shore. No matter if the Union or the Confederacy won, these notes would still be bankable.

Fairmount Academy's students and faculty posed for a photo outside the school in 1909. Principal Charles Myers is pictured at the far left. Next to him, from left, are teachers Lizzie Sudler, Rena Cox and Jeanette Chelton.

Following a number of years of oyster-shucking activity aboard the Ark, the area around it became covered by mountains of discarded oyster shells, making the boat inaccessible. Eventually the interior was also filled with discarded shells, putting an end to the area's first church, at least in practice. As of 1936, when the area was excavated for sewer installation, the Ark's superstructure still existed, buried beneath the "ground" made of oyster shells that comprise much of the foundation in the former area Somers Cove today.

New areas of the county began to thrive, as well. Steamboats traveled to Coulbourn Creek, which had developed into a maritime community in its own right. The village on the creek contained stores, a machine shop, a shipyard and an oyster packing plant. Further west, Potato Neck received its own school. Nicknamed the Potato Neck School, it is better known today by its proper name, Fairmount Academy. Established in what is now Upper Fairmount, in 1839, the current academy structure was built in the 1860s and served the area until it closed with the realignment of county schools in 1969.

By 1850 a handful of landowners had emerged as the wealthiest in the county. Chief amongst them was attorney John Woodland Crisfield, who had amassed the equivalent of $17,000 in land. Born near Chestertown in Kent County on November 8, 1806, Crisfield was one of the few college-educated residents of Somerset County. Having earned his degree from Washington College, he was admitted to the Maryland Bar in 1830 and moved to Princess Anne, where he became a prominent attorney.

Crisfield also was a strong politician, elected to serve Somerset in the Maryland House of Delegates in 1836. More than a decade later, in 1847, he was elected as a Whig to serve Maryland in the U.S. Congress, serving again from 1861 to 1863.

While Crisfield's holdings were large in 1850, many longtime Somerset landowners were watching their empires crumble. Much of the United States' earliest economy was based on the tobacco standard. Though that crop was not as popular in Eastern Shore Maryland as it was in neighboring states like Virginia, tobacco prices dictated what prices could be paid for other goods and services. As the tobacco crops dwindled elsewhere, so did the economy of Somerset County.

As some of the earliest landholders in the county sold off portions of their property to pay the bills, they needed—and could afford—fewer slaves. Many were emancipated outright. Some went to live in the "Maryland Colony in Africa," a portion of which is now Liberia, so nicknamed because of the preponderance of freed Maryland slaves residing in that area. Others remained in Somerset County. By 1850, freed slaves accounted for about half the county's African American population.

Crisfield was one of a number of pro-slave political leaders from the Eastern Shore who fought against the reapportionment of the Maryland General Assembly in 1850. The battle, if lost, would give Baltimore and Maryland's Western Shore counties more votes in the assembly than those of the Eastern Shore. When the struggle was over, the Eastern Shore delegation, which also included Somerset residents John Dennis, James Dennis, J.J. Dashiell and William Williams, lost. The number of assembly seats from the Eastern Shore shrank from forty to twenty-nine.

Attorney John Woodland Crisfield, namesake of the city of Crisfield, wore many hats throughout Somerset County's history. In addition to serving as president of the Eastern Shore Railroad, he also was elected a U.S. congressman under President Abraham Lincoln.

There had already been calls for secession of the Eastern Shore from the state of Maryland. Within months of the signing of the Declaration of Independence, Eastern Shore legislators were lobbying for a separation from the Maryland colony. A motion to do so filed by Delegate Turbott Wright was voted down 30–17.

By 1787, Shore officials were once again calling for separate rule. Non-Shore legislators tried to quell this idea by promising to hold every other session of the General Assembly on the Eastern Shore, in Easton. Those plans never came to fruition. In 1809, state legislators grudgingly recognized a new request, made in the form of the Eastern Shore Compact, that one of Maryland's two U.S. senators always be an Eastern Shore resident. Though said to be unconstitutional all along, the compact remained law until 1896.

While that gave the Shore some measure of perceived equality in national affairs, it did little to provide equity in state matters. In 1811, the General Assembly approved large sums to build Cumberland Pike and Chesapeake and Ohio Canal, and boost the upstart Baltimore and Ohio Railroad. None of these measures were of any perceived benefit to the Eastern Shore, and calls for secession started again.

In 1833, Governor C.P. Bennett of Delaware sought to take advantage of this division in interests to enhance his own state. He sent a letter to Governor George Howard of Maryland, proposing to take over operations of the Eastern Shore on behalf of Delaware. Newspapers at the time reported the governor also had his eye on Eastern Shore Virginia, though no formal action was taken to acquire that area.

Delegate Martin Wright filed a motion for a committee to consider Bennett's offer. Perhaps weary of the continual outcry of injustice from Shore residents, delegates amended the bill to offer a referendum and let voters on the Eastern Shore decide of which state they would rather be a part. The bill passed by a whopping 40–24 vote. However, the referendum never surfaced, being voted down by a marginal 5–4 in the State Senate.

In 1842, the cry arose again for a referendum that would allow the Eastern Shore to join Delaware. However, Maryland officials worried that would drain the state's tax base even further, and Delaware was in such dire financial straits itself that the idea of taking on nine more counties no longer seemed appealing. Again, the idea died.

Now, in 1850, Eastern Shore legislators were considering such a split once again. However, legislators turned down the request for a committee to study the matter, putting a quick end to the Shore's final secession attempt of the nineteenth century. Still, Crisfield was not done with his attempts to push the beliefs of the Eastern Shore—and Somerset County—above those of the rest of the state, including the increasingly unpopular notion of owning slaves.

Between 1850 and 1860, the number of plantation owners in Somerset dwindled from 170 to just 90. Onetime paid farmhands were now seeking other occupations, becoming coopers, tanners, blacksmiths and carpenters. Still, their toils were nothing compared to those Somerset slaves who had worked most of the same farms. Many were sold to Southern landowners, who put them to work in fields growing and picking the United States' next big cash crop, cotton.

Such was likely the case of the slave woman Grace and her eleven-month-old son sold by Thomas Sudler at the courthouse in Princess Anne on September 6, 1853. Owned by Sudler's deceased cousin, Grace had been placed in the jail at Princess Anne to curtail any escape plans.

At noon that day, Edward Wainwright, the town auctioneer, sold Grace and her son to the slave firm Woolfolk, Sanders and Overly of Baltimore. From there she probably was taken to the firm's slave jail in Baltimore before being transported to New Orleans, where she would have been sold to a plantation owner in Louisiana or Mississippi, fetching about $800. Market prices for slaves in New Orleans and Richmond about that time ranged from $350 for young girls to $1,300 for the healthiest full-grown men.

As these prices rose, slavery was once again in vogue throughout Somerset County and much of Maryland's Eastern Shore. Though slave imports were banned in the United States in 1808, slave smugglers enjoyed a booming trade. In the mid-1800s, many new slaves to Somerset County came from the Caribbean area, including Trinidad, Tobago, Antigua and Barbados. Many practiced "hoodoo," a variation of voodoo strange to the local plantation owners of the day.

The duties of these slaves were not confined only to the fields. When work was light, they were hired out to other industries, including shipping. Slaves loaded the bulk of the lumber transported from coastal Somerset towns, including Somers Cove and areas now encompassed by modern-day Salisbury. They also were loaned as apprentices to former farmhands now plying other trades or put on duty as pig herders, tending the large masses of pigs that once occupied the county's pine forests.

For this labor, many Somerset slaves of this era were given small parcels of plantation land on which to grow their own crops or raise chickens. They traded vegetables and eggs with townspeople, especially in the Princess Anne area, for rations or small amounts of money. They also sold molasses candy in churches, especially during the holidays, or illegally hired themselves out to perform odd jobs. Some even made money by joining Somerset's amateur boxing circuit.

Following the 1831 Virginia slave rebellion led by Nat Turner, Somerset citizens had placed fairly strict sanctions on their own slaves in hopes of preventing a similar incident locally. Church bells in Princess Anne rang at nine o'clock in the evening in the winter and ten o'clock in the evening in summer, signaling curfew for African Americans. Local law-enforcement agencies or community militias were at liberty to arrest any African Americans, free or slave, after the appointed hour. The sale of alcoholic beverages to African Americans also was illegal in Somerset County.

The fear of slave rebellion came to a head in the county in October 1859, when news of a slave raid—led by John Brown in Harper's Ferry, Virginia—produced rumors of similar upheaval in Somerset. Armed citizens patrolled the streets for signs of insurgence and searched slave quarters and the homes of free African Americans for weapons. A slave suspected of potential rebellion was killed.

In reality, slave rebellion in Somerset County was not marked by violence, but by work slowdowns on the job and illnesses faked during the middle of harvesting seasons. The Underground Railroad helped some escape north through Delaware, few obstacles standing in their way once they passed the slave agents in Seaford. Several Somerset homes, possibly including Teackle Mansion, allegedly had connections with the Underground Railroad, though many of those connections are little more than speculation today.

By 1960, the number of free African Americans in Somerset County had increased to 4,483. This largely outnumbered the slave owners in the county at that time, which were only 747. Somerset's free African American community collectively held more than $23,500 in wealth—according to the 1860 U.S. Census—working as farmhands (who typically earned 50¢ per day plus board), blacksmiths, carpenters, laborers and watermen. Their annual salary was an average $100. In exchange for living in the county, they were required to donate three days of labor annually to help maintain roads.

One of the most prosperous free African Americans in Somerset at this time was the Reverend Frost Pollitt, who oversaw the Methodist Episcopal Church in Princess Anne. A circuit preacher, his messages touting a future of freedom and equity for all Americans regardless of color riled officials in Accomack County, where he was arrested in 1856. Other prosperous, free Somerset African Americans on record in the 1850s and early 1860s include woodcutter George Ballard, waterman Raymond Miles and farmer George Green.

These African Americans rose through much hardship to be called "prosperous." In 1858, Maryland delegates from Somerset, Worcester, Talbot and Caroline Counties banded together to form a platform that would require all free African Americans in Maryland to re-enter slavery or leave the state.

The next January, the Jacobs Bill was introduced into the Maryland General Assembly, offering a plan to re-enslave all free African Americans with less than $150 in personal wealth. Somerset supported the bill during a statewide referendum in November 1859, though its citizens were in the minority.

At this time Somerset was one of the poorest counties in Maryland, and indeed on the Eastern Shore—only Caroline County was poorer. Manufacturing businesses included nine flour and meal mills and twenty-two sawmills. Sales of goods averaged just $200,000 annually, and laborers who earned the most were bricklayers at about $3 per day, followed by carpenters at $1 per day. Clearly Somerset was a blue-collar county, with the average person holding just $346 in land and goods by the 1860 census.

Farming was the top occupation in the county at that time. Annual harvests included corn (606,000 bushels in 1860), wheat (138,000 bushels) and honey (16,000 pounds). Somerset farmers also raised more than 16,000 hogs that year. Wholesale prices for wheat at brokerages in Baltimore netted the farmers an average of 97¢ per bushel of wheat and 55¢ per bushel of corn.

Retail, Somerset residents could expect to pay about 4¢ per pound for flour, between 8 and 9¢ per pound for sugar and bacon, 25¢ for a peck of Irish potatoes, 37¢ per gallon of molasses and 23¢ per pound of butter. In contrast, a good pair of shoes could set a worker back $1.75. Most in the county who did not farm were in some way connected to the shipping industry, which saw boats leave almost daily from Somers Cove, Newtown (now Pocomoke), Deal Island and Barren Springs (now Mardela Springs) loaded with goods for the West Indies.

Regardless of the trades plied, most Somerset County residents who were eligible to vote were greatly interested in politics. Few had seen a more heated election in their lifetimes than the presidential ballot of 1860. Once all the votes were counted, Constitutional Unionist John Bell won in Somerset with 1,636 votes. Southern Democrat John Breckinridge followed closely with 1,339. Stephen Douglas trailed with only 89 votes, and Republican Abraham Lincoln came in dead last with only 2 votes.

Nationally, the vote was completely reversed, and Lincoln emerged as the victor. Though this likely did not endear the people of Somerset County to the federal government, it caused many more worries among states south of Maryland, where landowners feared the Republican Party would destroy slavery. Bolstered by the secession of South Carolina shortly after the election, Southern states began voting one by one to leave the Union and form their own country, the Confederate States of America. By February 1, 1861, Mississippi, Florida, Alabama, Georgia, Louisiana and Texas had officially left the Union.

As early as December 1860, Major A.H. Handy, a Somerset native who had moved to Mississippi and subsequently become a wealthy land and slave owner, was touring Maryland, encouraging its people to secede, as well. The Confederacy, he said, would lift tariffs, allowing Marylanders to purchase goods from Europe at costs cheaper than the Union states. The Southern states, where most open land was used to grow cotton, also would provide an open marketplace for Maryland agriculture and livestock, Handy said. In Somerset, Maryland delegates James Dennis and Edward Long vowed to work for recognition of the new government.

However, they did not count on the staunch opposition of John Crisfield, who fought for Maryland to remain in the Union. If Maryland joined the Confederacy, he reasoned, it would be one of the first points of attack from the more powerful Northern Union states. If Maryland remained a Union ally, however, its timber and agriculture would be of great use to the Northern states, and the Eastern Shore's landowners and manufacturers could turn an even greater profit.

Though his reasons may have been less than charitable, Crisfield was noted as the most outspoken political leader in favor of the Union during a peace conference called between Union and Confederate states in Washington, D.C., on February 1, 1861, the very day Texas voted to secede. The conference failed, and the Civil War began just two months later with the April 15 Confederate attack on Fort Sumter, South Carolina.

Of special interest during these early war actions was Maryland, which federal officials feared might side with the Confederacy. State leaders who seemed most likely to call for secession—including Long and Dennis, Major Handy's operatives in Somerset County—were placed under national surveillance. On September 16, 1861, both Long and Dennis were arrested by federal marshals as Confederate sympathizers and imprisoned at Fort McHenry in Baltimore.

That same month, President Lincoln was introduced to another Somerset County native, Anna Ella Carroll. Born August 19, 1815, Carroll was the daughter of Somerset

County aristocrat and one-time Maryland Governor Thomas King Carroll, who built his ornate home, Kingston Hall, in the county between 1780 and 1783. However, as landholdings crumbled in Somerset County in the mid-1800s, so did the Carroll family's. Thomas sold Kingston Hall and moved to a more modest home in neighboring Dorchester County.

Anna did not go with him. Instead, she set out to make a name for herself writing for newspapers, especially on the activities of the railroads. Gravitating toward politics, she found herself in Washington, D.C., where she made good friends in President Millard Fillmore, Lincoln presidential opponent John Breckinridge and future Confederate President Jefferson Davis. In fact, Davis commissioned Carroll to study the Memphis-Charleston Railroad, a project that later helped her realize the importance of the railroad in maintaining the Confederate cause.

In the mid-1850s, Carroll raised money to help prevent her father's former slaves from being brokered by slave traders. Unlike her father, she felt slavery was immoral. During this time she also served as a record keeper for the failing Whig party. Through this service, she became privy to what may well have been the first secession proposal in the United States.

During the 1860 election, Carroll was not a Lincoln supporter. However, through her friendship with Republican leader William Henry Seward, she realized the consequences that could materialize, especially for slaves, if Lincoln lost the Civil War. In September 1861, she published the pamphlet *The War Powers of the Government*, throwing her journalistic fame behind Lincoln's actions. He requested a second pamphlet, and she complied with *The Relation of Revolted Citizens to the National Government*, an even more compelling propaganda piece.

Soon, she took on an even more integral role in Lincoln's war, serving as a spy for the Union in St. Louis, where she had family. Through this surveillance, she determined that a planned Union attack against the Confederates on the Mississippi River would not be successful. Instead, she recommended sending Union gunboats into the Tennessee River Valley, where they could overtake the Confederates and seize the Memphis and Charleston Railroad. The U.S. War Department followed this advice and found success in the plan. For her efforts, Carroll has been called an unofficial member of Lincoln's cabinet.

Like Carroll, the contributions of several other Somerset County natives to the Civil War were not necessarily produced on Somerset soil. General Arnold Elzey, born in 1816 at the Elmwood plantation on the Manokin River and graduating from the U.S. Army Academy at West Point in 1837, earned high accolades for his efforts during the Mexican-American War and the army's efforts against the Seminoles in Florida before renouncing his ties to the Union immediately following the attack on Fort Sumter.

Serving with General Thomas "Stonewall" Jackson, Elzey was promoted to major general in 1864 and charged with defending Richmond, Virginia, against the Union army. He later served with General John Hood in Georgia as part of the army of Tennessee. He resigned his post to Union soldiers following the capture of Jefferson Davis in 1865.

Another Somerset native playing an integral role in the Confederacy, General John Winder had been Elzey's professor at West Point. Stationed at Richmond, the sixty-one-year-old soldier was named commander of Union prisoners there. By 1862, this task grew to overseeing law and order in the city, and Winder used the charge to not only punish, but rehabilitate lawbreakers, assigning them to public works chain gangs.

Within the next two years, Winder was assigned to oversee several Confederate prisoner of war camps, including Libby Prison, Belle Isle Camp and Danville in Virginia. However, perhaps his most infamous assignment came in 1864, as he was promoted to command all Confederate prisoner of war camps east of the Mississippi River, including Andersonville in Georgia. This camp alone saw more than thirty-two thousand prisoners, with thousands more in the other prisons under Winder's command.

Later that year, when prisoner exchanges broke down between Union and Confederate camps under the assumption that returning Confederate soldiers would only strengthen the rebel cause, conditions at Andersonville deteriorated. Without enough food for his own troops, let alone prisoners, Winder became the scorn of many Northern newspapers. When he passed away in February 1865, many Unionists said they would rather he had died at the gallows than of natural causes.

Closer to home, Confederate support was also strong. On July 24, 1860, the Tyaskin Guard, Twenty-fifth Regiment, Somerset's first Confederate unit, was formed under the command of Captain John Moore. Within the next year, the county outfitted two more Confederate units: the Somerset Guard, commanded by Captain John W. Polk in the Twenty-fifth Regiment, and the Somerset Life Guard Dragoons, commanded by Captain Andrew Crawford in the Ninth Regiment.

By and large, however, Somerset's loyalties remained to the Union, probably by force more than anything else. In fall 1861, General John Dix, commander of the Maryland Department of the Union army, sent General Henry Lockwood to Cambridge in Dorchester County to serve as a base for anti-Confederate activity on the Eastern Shore. Lockwood quickly dispatched a unit down the Nanticoke River to shut down the Tyaskin Guard. He also ordered two companies of Union troops from Delaware sailing aboard the steamship *Balloon* to disembark at Whitehaven and march eight miles to Princess Anne to disarm the local militia for fear its members may have had Confederate sympathies.

That November, Purnell's Legion, a unit under the command of Baltimore postmaster and Worcester County native William Purnell in the Fourth Regiment, campaigned through Somerset County to stop Virginia Confederates from stuffing the Maryland ballot boxes during a special election.

Meanwhile, General Dix sent a patrol of government steamboats and tugboats through the Chesapeake to seek out boats smuggling goods to Confederate troops. One of the patrol's first seizures was a boat captained by Rehobeth waterman Greenleaf Johnson, sailing near Smith Island with a cargo of shoes. Charges were later dismissed when no proof could be offered that the shoes actually were bound for Confederate sale. History has shown that Johnson likely did indeed smuggle footwear to the Confederates, just as others from Somerset made a profit selling coffee and salt to the Southern troops.

In spring 1862, the U.S. Navy took matters into its own hands, staffing the bay with the gunboat *Hercules*. This boat captured several Deal Island-based ships that had smuggled goods to Confederates, including *Algonquin* and *Chesapeake*. A third, *Victory*, was captured off the coast of Virginia and burned.

Other Union ships, including *Reliance* and *Yankee*, soon joined the patrol, guided by lightships so they could better see enemy boats at night. On February 25, 1865, 150 Confederate soldiers invaded Smith Island, intent on destroying the lightships docked there. Crewmen aboard *Yankee* quickly detected the invaders, and they beat a hasty retreat, though several remained stranded on the island, where they later accepted Union capture over the conditions they faced there with neither food nor supplies.

During the war, each county in Maryland had a quota for supplying soldiers for the Union cause. By summer 1862, Somerset had reached only 157 of its 660-man quota. A draft system was quickly put into place. However, avoiding the draft was fairly easy. For an average of $105, a draftee could purchase a substitute to serve in his place. Some residents even imported Irish immigrants specifically for this purpose.

As the war grew bloodier, however, the price for a substitute increased to as much as $500, and those who could not afford the steeper price often fled the county, if not the state, to avoid conscription. Others took proactive measures, burning the crops of local Union draft officers. Many of the draftees and substitutes from Somerset were stationed at Camp Bradford, just south of Princess Anne. The encampment soon earned a local reputation even worse than the Confederates its men were supposed to be fighting.

However, that is not to say Somerset did not field any willing candidates for the Union cause. In December 1861, Captain Littleton Long, Hance Lawson and William Porter organized a military unit in Princess Anne as part of the First Regiment of Maryland's Eastern Shore Infantry. Company K, as the unit was named, was formed to protect Somerset from the threat of Confederates. Yet, rarely did the unit actually serve in Somerset.

During their first mission, flushing the Confederates out of Dover, Delaware, the unit's men earned the same reputation as Camp Bradford would the next year, proving themselves a drunken, rowdy bunch. Other assignments continued to take them away from their home county.

In 1863, shortly before the Battle of Gettysburg, General Lockwood received orders to congregate all units under his command, including Company K, to become part of the Union army of the Potomac. Many members of Company K—by then encamped in Cambridge—balked, saying they had joined the army to protect Somerset County, not fight battles in places about which they did not care. In all, sixty-one earned dishonorable discharges for the mutiny.

Camp Upton, a second Somerset Union base, was located in Salisbury at what is now the corner of U.S. 13 Business and Carroll Street. With orders to secure not only Somerset County, but the entire lower Eastern Shore against Confederate occupation, its troops earned reputations much nobler than those at Camp Bradford or the majority of Company K.

Throughout Company K's existence, John Crisfield was still fighting his own war with the federal government. No fan of secession, he lobbied hard for slavery to remain

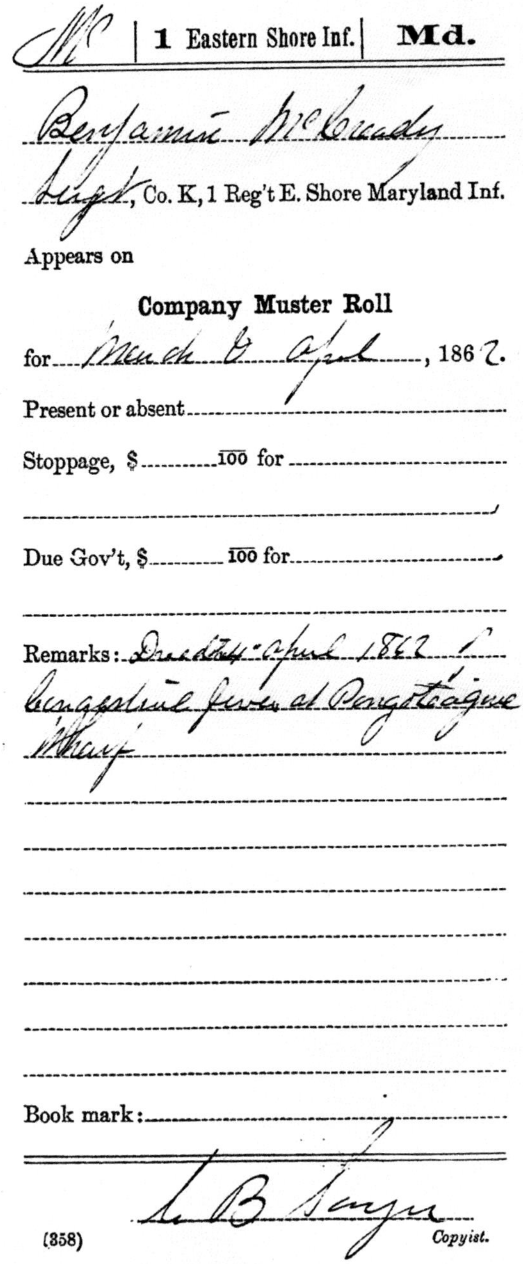

Mc | 1 Eastern Shore Inf. | Md.

Benjamin McCready

Sergt, Co. K, 1 Reg't E. Shore Maryland Inf.

Appears on

Company Muster Roll

for March & April, 1862.

Present or absent

Stoppage, $ 100 for

Due Gov't, $ 100 for

Remarks: Died 4th April 1862 of congestive fever at Pungoteague Wharf

Book mark:

L. B. Sayer

(358) *Copyist.*

This Civil War muster roll from the First Regiment of Maryland's Eastern Shore Infantry reports the death of soldier Benjamin McCready on April 4, 1862. McCready, who served with Somerset County's Company K, died of congestive fever at Pungoteague, Virginia.

legal. On December 16, 1861, a congressional bill introduced to emancipate slaves in Washington, D.C., told Crisfield he was losing that war. In March 1862, Lincoln sent for Crisfield to discuss expanding emancipation to Maryland.

During their discussion, Crisfield argued that slavery was actually better for the slaves than the conditions they would face on their own in the impoverished, war-torn country. Following that summer's passage of the Second Confiscation Act, which sanctioned the Union enlistment of African American soldiers and forbade the Union military from capturing runaway slaves, Lincoln and Crisfield met again. During this conference, in July 1862, Lincoln guaranteed Maryland slaveholders $300 for each slave emancipated and vowed to establish a colony specifically for freed Maryland slaves in Latin America. Again, Crisfield renounced the president's offer.

It didn't matter. Using the same promises the British Army had made to slaves during the Revolutionary War, Lincoln coaxed slaves in Maryland and other states to join the Union military, where they would be given freedom. The effects were felt on the Eastern Shore especially in 1863 and 1864 during the occupation of Colonel William Birney. Tasked by the U.S. War Department with freeing slaves on the Eastern Shore to join the Union army, Birney took his job seriously. During his first summer on the shore alone, he managed to free more than 200 slaves from Somerset and Worcester Counties, putting them aboard a steamboat at Snow Hill and promising them a better life in the military. Another 140 left Princess Anne to join that fall.

Though these actions incensed many in Somerset, others breathed a sigh of relief. Better their slaves be given the opportunity to march off to war then they be mandated to fight by force. Six of the slaves who left Somerset County in fall 1863 belonged to John Crisfield. The next year, he freed several more under the agreement that they serve in the war in place of his sons, who had been drafted. In total, some 270 Somerset slaves were freed to fight for the Union in 1864. One encampment of African American soldiers was even stationed in Somerset County, ostensibly to take on the home guard duties initially bestowed upon Company K.

This effectively ended the slave auctions that had become so popular at the county courthouse. If a slave was sold, all he had to do was offer then and there to sign with the Union army and be freed on the spot. The only Somerset slaves who did not have this option were those who were sent to live in slave prisons in Baltimore. But then, those slaves served no purpose to their masters since they were not around to work the fields. They were imprisoned on the principle of slavery.

By that time Crisfield, perhaps the Union's top spokesman on behalf of slavery, was out of office. His fall from power began in early 1863, when he accused Lincoln of promoting emancipation for his own benefit. The president, having grown tired of Crisfield's constant opposition, aligned his support with Henry Winter Davis, a Maryland anti-slavery leader who launched a statewide campaign to rid the government of pro-slavery candidates.

Prior to the 1863 election, Davis plotted with General Robert Schenck, a congressman from Ohio and commander of the War Department in Maryland, to issue General War Order 53, which mandated that all who cast votes were loyal to the Union and had never had contact with a member of the Confederacy. On Election Day, Schenck sent Union troops to all polling places on the Eastern Shore to ensure this order was carried out. Ballots were printed on two different colors of paper—yellow for anti-slavery candidates, white for pro-slavery candidates. Union troops in Somerset had orders to ensure the yellow ballots won.

Only one vote was cast in Princess Anne that day. It was cast by anti-slavery activist William Brittingham. The second person at the poll was Crisfield's own son, Arthur. Following harassment of the younger Crisfield by Union soldiers, Election Judge John Pinto ruled the election unlawful and closed the polling place. Federal troops arrested Pinto and Crisfield on the spot. Later, two other Somerset election judges, Levin Handy and W.W. Johnson, were also arrested for similar declarations.

Throughout the county, Union soldiers declared voters could choose only the yellow ballot. They hid the white ballots and threatened violence against those requesting white ballots. In some districts, voters fought back with gunfire. In the end, John Cresswell, Crisfield's anti-slavery opponent, won only by a slim margin, 6,742 to 5,482. Most conceded Crisfield likely would have won had it not been for the Union troops' involvement.

In April 1864, Somerset delegates prepared to join those from the rest of the state for a special constitutional convention in Annapolis for the purposes of instituting emancipation of slaves in Maryland. Somerset, perhaps the most pro-slave county left in the state, opposed the convention 1,331 to 813. Somerset delegate James Dennis was arrested as a Confederate supporter immediately prior to the convention and allowed to attend only after a fierce court battle. Somerset delegate Isaac Jones escaped arrest only due to his position as Maryland's attorney general.

It did not take long for the Somerset delegation to concede they would not win their battle to maintain slavery in Maryland. Instead, they sought the next-best deal, which in their mind was fair compensation for the slaves lost to emancipation. While they won that compensation at the state level, the federal government would not authorize funding for the initiative. In all, Maryland slaveholders lost an estimated $30 million to emancipation.

However, that was not the worst news for Somerset residents. In addition to calling for emancipation, the amended Maryland constitution now mandated public education be made available to all state residents, a stipulation the Somerset delegation feared would be used to educate emancipated slaves and disrupt the social structure of the Eastern Shore. Additionally, House of Delegates seats for the Eastern Shore and Southern Maryland would be reduced from thirty-four to a combined total of just seventeen. Western Shore counties would have unquestionable majority power in Maryland.

Somerset residents voted down the amended constitution 2,066 to 464. Statewide, however, the constitution was ratified 30,174 to 29,799. The Civil War would officially end the next year, in 1865. In Somerset County, however, the war was already over. Somerset had lost.

Chapter 6

Tracks Across the County

Though John Crisfield's national political career ended with the crooked election of 1863, his most important achievements in Somerset County were just beginning. In 1860, he lobbied the General Assembly for $112,000 in state funds to complete the proposed Eastern Shore Railroad from Cape Charles, Virginia, to Delmar, Delaware.

The idea for the railroad actually began in 1835 when another Somerset luminary, Dennis Littleton Teackle, founded plans for the line as the Eastern Shore Railroad's first president. Charged with raising $255,000 in stock, Teackle was well on his way to making the railroad a reality when his fortunes once again took a turn for the worse.

Having seen the benefits of railroads for shipping in New York and New England, Crisfield believed the iron horse was the key to raising the Eastern Shore's economic fortunes. He and several business partners purchased the bankrupt, unfinished railroad from Teackle's group for just that purpose. However, when war broke out in 1861, the idea of extending the rails into the lower Eastern Shore died.

Now that the war was over and Crisfield was out of office, he was free to resume his railroad plans. As president of the corporation, he spent most of 1863 and 1864 gathering rights of way so his workers could lay tracks stretching the Delmarva Peninsula. Sometimes special concessions were in order. John Horsey, for example, asked that the train station placed on his property be named in honor of his daughter, Marion. The town took on the resulting name of Marion Station.

Early stops along the railroad included most major towns of the time. However, the southernmost terminus in Maryland was somewhat of a mystery. Crisfield directed the tracks to be run into the Somerset County fishing village of Somers Cove, all the way down to the village's steamboat wharf.

Crisfield's theory was that this would allow steamboats to unload their shipments of produce directly onto freight trains, which could then carry the vegetables throughout the peninsula. Similarly, goods shipped by train could easily be loaded onto steamboats for delivery throughout the eastern seaboard and even abroad. What Crisfield may or may not have realized at the time was that these trains also would benefit the village's blossoming seafood industry.

The first train came to Somers Cove, the final portion of the railroad to be completed, on November 4, 1866. So pleased were citizens of the village with this development

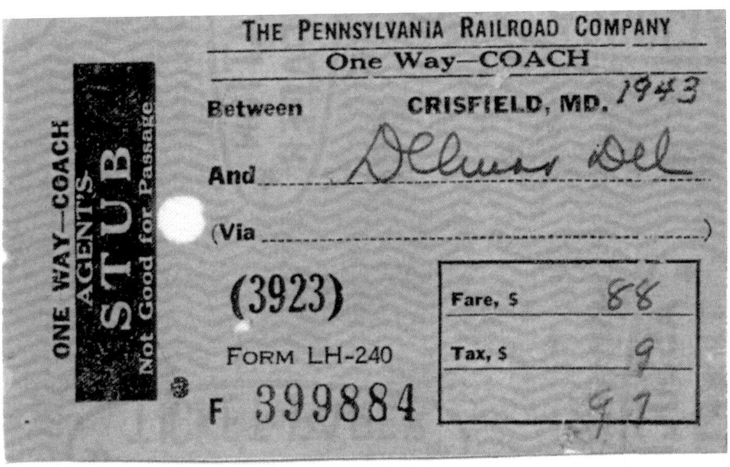

ONE WAY—COACH
AGENT'S
STUB
Not Good for Passage

THE PENNSYLVANIA RAILROAD COMPANY
One Way—COACH

Between CRISFIELD, MD. 1943
And Delmar Del
(Via)

(3923)

FORM LH-240

F 399884

Fare, $	88
Tax, $	9
	97

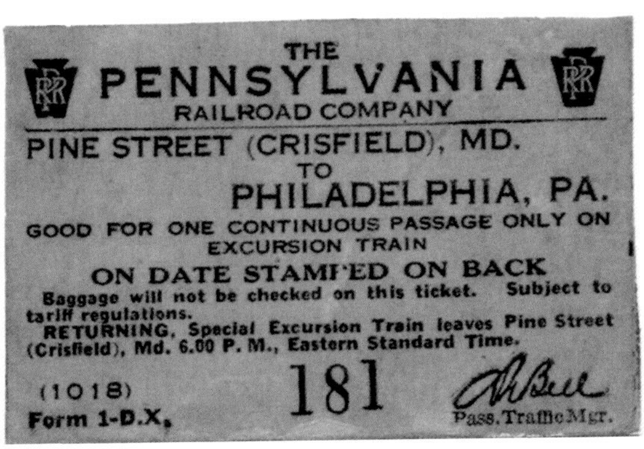

THE
PENNSYLVANIA
RAILROAD COMPANY

PINE STREET (CRISFIELD), MD.
TO
PHILADELPHIA, PA.

GOOD FOR ONE CONTINUOUS PASSAGE ONLY ON EXCURSION TRAIN
ON DATE STAMPED ON BACK
Baggage will not be checked on this ticket. Subject to tariff regulations.
RETURNING, Special Excursion Train leaves Pine Street (Crisfield), Md. 6.00 P. M., Eastern Standard Time.

(1018)
Form 1-D.X.
181
Pass. Traffic Mgr.

Above: A train pulls into Marion Station, named for Marion Horsey, daughter of the landowner who supplied property for the terminal. Railroads played an important part in Somerset County's economy from just after the Civil War until World War II.

Left: Trains in Somerset County were a popular means of passenger travel as well as freight shipping, evidenced by these Pennsylvania Railroad tickets from Crisfield.

that they renamed the area Crisfield in honor of the railroad's president. In 1872, the newly named Crisfield was incorporated into a city, comprised of Somers Cove and a large portion of Annemessex. At that time, however, the tracks still did not reach the steamboat wharf as Crisfield originally had intended. Instead, they stopped at Ward's Crossing, atop the last of the non-marshy soil. Any goods shipped from this station had to be taken there via horse and carriage.

Still, that early railroad accomplished its goal of growing the local populace. With easy access into the new city via the railroad, as well as plentiful job opportunities in the seafood industry, Crisfield's population soon boomed, as did water travel into the area. In 1867, the U.S. Lighthouse Service built a ten-thousand-dollar lighthouse near the entrance of the Little Annemessex River to guide boats into Crisfield. Later operated by the U.S. Coast Guard, the Somers Cove Lighthouse was put out of service and largely dismantled in 1932. Today, its remaining screwpile framework is still used as an unofficial navigational marker, earning it the nickname "Skeleton Lighthouse."

As the railroad brought new faces to Crisfield, new businesses quickly sprang up along the waterfront and inland areas in the form of saloons, gambling halls and brothels housed in shaky buildings on sometimes questionable, marshy ground. Finding drinking, fighting and prostitution as rampant as in the old west, Northerners moving to the area to tempt their fortunes in the seafood industry quickly dubbed Crisfield the "Dodge City of the East."

Perhaps the most infamous of all areas in Crisfield was Goodsell's Alley. John Goodsell was possibly the first property owner in Crisfield to determine that a good foundation could be built from otherwise worthless oyster shells, much as oyster shuckers had already been doing unintentionally in other parts of the city (such as the area around the Ark). He had train cars filled with shells delivered to his doorstep and commenced laying out a foundation for his own shucking house.

Goodsell's plan was to position his business along what was predicted to be Crisfield's Main Street. However, city planners had other ideas and moved the proposed Main Street one block to its present location. Furious, Goodsell unsuccessfully sued the city. He later moved out of the area.

However, that did not stop the violence in Goodsell's Alley. Instead, that honor went to Colonel Thomas Hodson, a local preacher, attorney and city commissioner. Rousted from his sleep one night by a fight in Goodsell's Alley, he reportedly grabbed his shotgun, pointed it from his second-story window facing the alley, and fired into the crowd. Though no injuries were reported, large-scale fights in the alley allegedly dwindled off shortly thereafter for fear that the preacher would shoot once again. In 1875, the Crisfield City Council passed a short-lived localized prohibition act in an attempt to quell the violence even more.

Goodsell's Alley still exists in Crisfield, though it is nowhere near as rowdy as it once was. In the early twenty-first century the most popular business there was an ice cream parlor. This is in sharp contrast to the businesses stationed there in Goodsell's day. They included a cigar stand operated by Will Horsey, Tucker's Saloon, Jim Tracey's saloon, a hardware store operated by George Holland, a boardinghouse for sailors run by Dallas

Built in 1867, the Somers Cove Lighthouse near the entrance of the Little Annemessex River helped guide boats into Crisfield until discontinuing service in 1932.

This early photo of Main Street shows a long-forgotten view of Upper Fairmount following Somerset's late 1800s property boom.

Somers and perhaps the most unusual shop in such a rough neighborhood, Candy Kitchen, a sweetshop owned by a Mrs. Cave.

One of the more positive aspects of the railroad's first years in Crisfield was that it drew enough new residents to the area to begin forming fraternal organizations. Goodsell himself was instrumental in the earliest of these organizations, Chesapeake Lodge 147 of the Ancient Free and Accepted Masons. Goodsell was the first master of this lodge in 1869. The area's first Masons met in his oyster house.

Goodsell also turned over his oyster house as a meeting place for Crisfield's second fraternal organization, the Knights of Pythias. Founded in 1871 as a friendly rival to the local Masons, the Knights were a part of Crisfield until disbanding about the time of World War II. The Knights' cause grew in Potato Neck, now Upper Fairmount, during the early 1870s, as well, as a hall for the organization was constructed next to Fairmount Academy in 1872.

With so many new residents moving to Crisfield in the 1870s, the city's water system was strained. During the Civil War, a windmill constructed in an area known as Kennerly's Wharf in what is today downtown Crisfield provided a primitive pump that would draw fresh water from the ground about two hundred feet below. The water was stored in a cypress tank and sold to the public at two cents per bucket. Water consumed on the premises allegedly was free. Captain Augustus Maddox operated the mill and reportedly made quite a nice living from water sales there.

Later, a second source of fresh water—an elevated tank built alongside what is now Maryland Avenue—was established to provide water to the steam engines that rumbled through the city. Local thirsty residents were allowed to come to the tank for a free glass—but not a whole bucket.

The railroad also brought about readership for several new newspapers in the county between 1866 and 1872. The *True Marylander* of Princess Anne, which later combined with the *Somerset Herald* to form the *Marylander and Herald* (known today as *Somerset Herald*), was first published in 1866. Crisfield saw its first paper about 1872 with the publication of the short-lived *Crisfield Index*. A more established paper, the *Crisfield Leader*, served the city from 1872 until about 1908, publishing under a variety of names in later years, including the *Somerset Republican* in 1904 and *Crisfield Tribune* in 1908.

One story—true or not—about Crisfield's early years that has been passed down through generations; in October 1874, while inspecting land for a proposed railroad extension to the steamboat wharf, John Crisfield stepped on a loose plank on a wooden ramp and fell into about fifteen feet of water. Local railroad agent John Lee Carman dove in and saved the former congressman, who could not swim. Upon pulling Crisfield to safety, Carman allegedly remarked that the city's name was official now that its namesake had been baptized in its waters.

A Philadelphia native and Civil War veteran with the Union army, Carman was as integral as John Crisfield to the success of the railroad in Crisfield. Joining the New York, Philadelphia and Norfolk Railroad Company in Camden, New Jersey, shortly after the war, he was among the first to oversee the railroad's freight trains as they rumbled over the tracks at Somers Cove. The company charged him with divining ways to increase its freight business at the new terminal.

His idea was to extend the rail line over the marsh and water to Old Island, a formidable task to be sure. The first step was to get the tracks extended to the steamboat wharf, which is exactly what he was encouraging John Crisfield to do at the time of his "baptism." Trains began rolling to the water's edge in the mid-1870s.

However, that was as far as the project would go. The powers that be in Crisfield and with the railroad determined that an extension to Old Island was economically unfeasible and ultimately unnecessary. The tracks at the steamboat wharf already allowed a direct connection between water and rail shipping, and that had been the goal all along. Still, Carman continued to champion the railroad until his death in 1914. In his enthusiasm he made one other prophecy that never quite came true: that Crisfield's population would reach fifty thousand. It topped out at about fifteen thousand.

While John Crisfield was busy laying railroad tracks to Somers Cove, events of a much different nature at the other end of the county literally were about to change the face of Somerset forever. For many of the same reasons Worcester County was formed from part of Somerset in 1742, Wicomico County was created in 1867 from portions of Somerset and Worcester. This time, the geographic change hinged on the city of Salisbury, which had straddled the Somerset-Wicomico border for more than a century.

In 1742, Salisbury was little more than a small town where travelers to the lower portions of Somerset could rest before continuing south. However, by the Civil War, Salisbury had grown into a considerable metropolis along the Wicomico River. With the advent of rail travel, it looked as if there would be no stopping growth in this town. Except it was still literally a town divided, between the two counties. The creation of Wicomico County allowed Salisbury, the new county seat, to blossom into one of the

The first building christened Crisfield High School, in 1908, is seen to the left in this early twentieth-century scene, overshadowed by its predecessor, Crisfield Academy.

largest communities on the Eastern Shore. With Wicomico now in place, Somerset took on the boundaries that still exist today.

Back in Crisfield, the city received its first academy, Crisfield Academy, in 1876, marking the beginning of formalized education. The building served students in all grades until 1908, when the first public Crisfield High School was built alongside the original academy on Asbury Avenue. The original academy building served as the city's first formal elementary school from 1908 to 1936. It was demolished in 1937.

The city's first school for African American children opened on Collins Street about 1880, serving the area through the early 1940s. Though it served only grades one through six during its earliest years, its faculty taught classes up through the eleventh grade—the highest grade offered anywhere in the county at the time—by the time a new African American high school was built just prior to World War II. The aging school on Collins Street saw its last students in 1951, shortly before the new school, Crisfield Colored High School, was enlarged to accommodate Crisfield's African American elementary school students, as well as the upper grades.

Indeed, Crisfield was a growing place in the late 1700s. However, it still retained much of its post-Civil War charm. In the June 1879 issue of *Harper's New Monthly Magazine*, correspondent Howard Pyle painted a scene of the city from that era:

> *A town of oysters built on oyster shells. Such is Crisfield. A man buys a building lot at the bottom of the harbor, and then purchases oyster shells enough to raise it above high-water mark...Back from Crisfield and surrounding it on this peninsula are thick glades of pine timber, alternated by brilliantly green stretches of flat meadow land covered with rank grass. The region back of town is very thickly settled by fishermen and oystermen, who choose the neighborhood out of such easy access to the water. The cottages stand every where, fronting in all directions, as though shaken from some enormous pepper caster, some along hard level roads that intersect this region, some back in the glades, some singly, some collected in a small nucleus around a cross-road store.*
>
> *Oysters, oysters, every where, in barrels, in boxes, in cans, in buckets, in the shell and out. But little business is carried on here except oystering; a little fishing and a little crabbing, perhaps, but nothing else. The railroad that runs through the length of the town, terminating at the steamboat wharf at the harbor, rests on a road bed of oyster shells, as firm and solid as can be desired.*

Many of the businessmen who had moved into lower Somerset County following the Civil War came hoping to make fortunes in the seafood industry. By 1878, oysters harvested in Crisfield topped out around three hundred thousand bushels, giving local packinghouse owners a profit of about $150,000, a fortune in the late nineteenth century. This would come to be considered a poor season based on the numbers that soon followed.

Chapter 7

Bounty on the Chesapeake

By 1872, Crisfield had already proven itself the oyster capital of Maryland, with some six hundred registered boats in that port dredging and tonging (pulling up oysters with tongs) for the popular mollusk that year. That was nothing compared to the city's harvest during the 1880s. The oyster bounty on the Chesapeake and in Tangier Sound, in particular, was so great that the city saw a seafood rush akin to the California gold rush thirty years before.

Just as with miners during the gold rush, Somerset watermen were quick to react to "claim jumpers"—out-of-state dredgers and tongers who made off with oysters from Somerset oyster beds. As early as 1820, Maryland officials heard claims that New England watermen were coming into the Chesapeake and "stealing" oysters the locals believed belonged only to the people of Maryland. State legislators formed an "oyster navy" in 1867 to help defend local oyster beds from out-of-state poachers.

By the time the oyster industry reached its peak in the 1880s, however, many local watermen were more than ready to take matters into their own hands to defend their livelihoods. One major problem was that for centuries, no clear boundary line had been drawn between Maryland and Virginia waters in the Chesapeake Bay. On the line were forty square miles of oyster breeding grounds in Tangier Sound, as well as part of the Little Annemessex River.

On June 1, 1872, officials from both states met in Crisfield to determine the boundary once and for all. With so much at stake, neither side was willing to negotiate, and talks quickly broke down. The boundary line would not be settled until 1877, when officials found largely in Virginia's favor. This did not sit well with Somerset watermen, who risked having their boats confiscated—or even risked being killed outright—by continuing to harvest oysters in the once-disputed territory. Virginia watermen were only too glad to return the favor by stalking Somerset waters.

Following an unsuccessful appeal to Maryland's oyster navy in December 1883, a group of Crisfield shucking house owners including Isaac Lawson and L.T. Dryden set out to stop the poaching the only way they knew how—through gunfire. Bullets blazed across the Chesapeake as both Maryland and Virginia residents fired upon each other to protect their precious oyster beds.

The ongoing battle came to a head when Captain A.J. Read, aboard the Virginia Police schooner *Tangier*, spied watermen aboard a Smith Island vessel illegally harvesting oysters in Virginia waters. Such poachers from both sides would come to be called "oyster pirates." Chasing the Maryland boat back to Smith Island, Read came under the fire of about twenty-five civilian guns. Returning fire with his ship's cannon, Read knew he was outnumbered. The Smith Islanders quickly set up a makeshift fortress against the cannon fire, and Read was forced to retreat back to Virginia. So went the fabled "oyster wars" of the Chesapeake Bay.

By 1885, two years after a fire destroyed much of downtown Crisfield, the oyster catch began to level off in the area. Still, the city's packinghouses were shucking an annual average of four hundred thousand bushels, now dredged in the rivers as well as the bay. Seafood plants destroyed in the fire were quickly rebuilt, their owners reluctant to miss out on any more of the seafood boom than they had to. More than three thousand were employed through some aspect of the oyster industry. Packers at the larger firms were paid as much as $3.50 per day for twenty gallons shucked.

Payment was made in the form of metal tokens called "checks," imprinted with the packinghouse's name or company initials and a number referencing the number of gallons an individual worker shucked that day. The tokens were turned in, in return for payment of the day's established shucking rate.

The average wholesale rate for a bushel of oysters by this time was about 25¢. Each bushel of unshucked oysters equaled about a gallon once shucked. Selling for about $1.00 per gallon, this meant a profit of 50¢ or more per bushel for packinghouse owners. Unscrupulous packers often padded these gallons with ice and oyster liquor, the juice found inside oyster shells once the meat was removed. A "gallon of oysters" seldom actually constituted a gallon of just oysters.

Meanwhile, the oyster wars continued. In 1885, African American watermen reported they were being forced off the Nanticoke by oyster pirates from other states. One of the biggest changes the oyster industry brought about in Somerset County was a shift in perception regarding the status of African Americans. Many oyster plant owners originally were from the North, where sympathies toward African Americans ran high, even before the Civil War.

As profits were made, local packers and watermen began to share their views, accepting that African American workers in packinghouses and on the water were essential to keeping the industry alive. Those who controlled the oyster controlled politics in Somerset County. The respect African American watermen received from their Caucasian colleagues was a sharp contrast to the conditions many faced just twenty years earlier.

Watermen from Potato Neck responded to the call for help on the Nanticoke, setting up a cannon to blast the pirates out of the region. Sometimes, however, authorities were still called in lieu of vigilantism. In January 1886, the police boat *Kent* of the Maryland oyster navy received notification from Somerset watermen that oyster pirates had been spotted in local waters. Spying *Kent* bearing down on them, the pirates opened fire. Shots flew back and forth, resulting in several deaths.

Wenona Harbor was filled with workboats circa 1900, their captains hoping to obtain their share of the seafood fortune available in Somerset's waters. *Courtesy Cindy Powell.*

Even the threat of death did not deter most oyster pirates, however. They just developed new tricks. One common ploy was to coat their sails with mud and plunder at night in an effort not to be detected.

Integral to the oyster harvests of the late nineteenth century were the boats watermen sailed throughout the Chesapeake Bay.

One such craft, developed in the 1880s, was the bugeye. Several theories exist as to how this boat received its unique name. Whether its moniker derived from its design, which resembled a bug when viewed from the front; the Scottish word for oyster shell, "buckie"; or the folkloric notion that it could turn "on a bug's eye" remains lost to history.

What is known about the bugeye is that it was much more maneuverable than the earliest oyster vessel, the pungy. Weighing in at as much as sixty-nine tons, pungies were much bulkier than bugeyes, yet preferred by most oyster dredgers until the 1880s due to their sheer power. While pungies resembled miniature sailing ships, bugeyes were flat-bottomed, weighing as little as three tons. Its aft cabin and smooth bottom allowed them to draw less water, making them ideal for navigating shallow waters where oysters had not yet been overharvested.

Quite a few bugeyes plying the Chesapeake at that time came from shipbuilders in Somerset County. One of the most notable was John Branford of Potato Neck, who is known to have produced at least twenty-five of the vessels from the early 1880s through about 1911. Much less expensive than pungys, bugeyes in the 1880s cost about $1,150.

Perhaps the most majestic workboat produced during this time was the legendary Chesapeake Bay skipjack. The V-bottomed boat with the large mainsail has over time become the ship most often connected with the romantic days of oystering on the bay.

Inexpensive to buy and easier to operate than either pungys or bugeyes, they were the most common working craft on the Chesapeake by 1901, about a decade following their introduction.

Dozens of these boats were constructed in Somerset County in shipyards in Crisfield, Potato Neck (later Fairmount), Oriole and Deal Island. They held a special cultural significance in Deal Island. For years, unofficial workboat races were held in Somerset's waterfront communities as those not selling their daily catch to buy boats—vessels sent by packinghouses to purchase oysters from watermen still on the bay—sped inland to be the first to sell to packers.

In the 1920s and early 1930s, however, the races devolved from necessity into contests for bragging rights. In 1921, the (Baltimore) *Sun* started sponsoring workboat races in Maryland. Each boat raced against others in its class, pungys against pungys, bugeyes against bugeyes, skipjacks against skipjacks. In 1959, the watermen of Deal Island began reminiscing about these races. The last one anyone could remember took place in 1931. Some sought to rekindle the spirit by hosting an annual skipjack race. The idea caught on like wildfire.

The first modern Deal Island skipjack race took place in 1960. Five years later, skipjack races in Annapolis became part of an annual statewide Chesapeake Appreciation Day, underscoring their importance in Maryland's legacy. In 1969, *Sports Illustrated* called the Chesapeake Appreciation Day event, held the last Saturday in October, the largest annual sailing race in the nation. Though the Appreciation Day events are no longer held, skipjack races remain an integral part of Deal Island, where they are held each year on Labor Day.

Somerset County's skipjack heritage runs deep. The largest such vessel ever built, *Robert L. Webster*, was constructed in Oriole by shipwright Sylvester Muir. The thirty-five-ton boat spanned sixty feet from stern to bow. In Deal Island, a Miss Skipjack beauty queen is chosen annually. One of the main qualifications is that all contestants must have at least one ancestor who captained a skipjack.

However, the majestic boats are a dying breed. By 1977, only thirty-six working skipjacks still existed on the bay. Those remaining were named to the National Register of Historic Places in 1985. In 2002, the national register upgraded the skipjacks' status to "endangered." By then, fewer than a dozen remained.

In the late 1800s, oysters were the undisputed champions of the seafood industry in Somerset County. Crisfield alone boasted so many crews intent on cashing in on the mollusk that one allegedly could walk across the harbor aboard workboat decks. However, that does not mean oysters were the only Chesapeake Bay harvest of which people were taking note. In fact, one man used his marketing expertise to turn his family's name into a brand dedicated to one of the area's most unusual delicacies—terrapin.

Albert LaVallette Jr. was a schooner captain in 1887 when he heard stories about the plethora of diamondback terrapin in the Chesapeake Bay, especially the portion of it around Crisfield. Once considered a food suitable only for commoners and slaves (a mid-1800s law prohibited slave owners from serving the meal more than thrice weekly), terrapin was about to take off in the world of fine dining.

Workboats docked at Deal Island in this 1920s photo exemplified the importance of the seafood industry on Somerset's economy during the first two-thirds of the twentieth century.

The captain staked out a large parcel of land in Crisfield that still bears his family name, building terrapin pens near his home. Once enclosed, the terrapin would thrive off the crab scraps LaVallette fed them. The more the terrapin grew, the more they would bring at market.

Many thought LaVallette was crazy. After all, terrapin were as plentiful as grass and only slightly tastier. However, the shrewd marketer had a plan. He created a recipe chock-full of spices to hide the actual terrapin flavor. He then traveled to the largest cities in the eastern United States—New York, Philadelphia, Baltimore and Washington, D.C., and convinced exactly one upscale restaurant in each of those cities to buy his recipe.

Suddenly, demand for terrapin skyrocketed. After all, if the recipe was so secretive only a half dozen or so select restaurants in the entire country had the rights to sell LaVallette terrapin soup, it must have been good! And no one could make LaVallette soup without genuine LaVallette terrapin.

Almost overnight, the price of the terrapin skyrocketed. The once-worthless creatures suddenly were selling for up to three dollars each. And that was just to LaVallette, who turned around and sold them to his handful of carefully selected restaurants at one dollar per underside inch. The restaurants passed the gouging onto their customers, who happily paid five dollars or more per bowl for the soup, a hefty price in the late 1890s.

By about 1912, the terrapin industry began lagging, a victim of illegal overfishing. The going rate at the time was seven dollars per terrapin. The species continued in diminished numbers, though America's taste for terrapin eventually tapered off. By 1926, the Crisfield pounds that once held hundreds of thousands of terrapin now boasted only about ten thousand at a time. Watermen had given up on the harvest, as it was nearly impossible to make a living catching a species that was practically endangered.

Most local terrapins at that time were captured by local youngsters and sold a few at a time to local terrapin farmers for pocket change. Once fattened with crab scraps, these terrapin sold for about twenty-five dollars a dozen wholesale, forty dollars retail, and averaged between six and eight inches long. Many were sold by the barrelful at deep discounts. By the 1950s, terrapin were all but extinct, and the industry died out completely.

Through careful conservation, however, Maryland officials were able to nurse the population back to good health. In 2002, the state's first official terrapin sanctuary, named in honor of Governor Parris Glendening, was dedicated at Janes Island State Park in Crisfield.

Another unique industry in Crisfield based on the bay's bounty in the late 1800s was menhaden fishing. In 1871, local businessmen L.E.P. Dennis and R.H. Mulligan established a menhaden fertilizer factory on Old Island. Crews manned the company's large fishing schooners with purse nets, hauling in menhaden by the thousands in the Chesapeake Bay and along the Atlantic coast. At the day's end, the fish were loaded onto small boats and taken back to the factory for processing.

In 1892, Mulligan sold his interest in the company to Dennis, who operated it as the family business L.E.P. Dennis and Son. Most of the workers at the factory actually lived on the island itself, either in homes with their families or in a bunkhouse built for the single, mostly immigrant, employees. The factory itself burned and was rebuilt in 1900. That same year, Dennis replaced the fishing schooners with four steamboats—*Amagansett, E. Benson Dennis, Luce Brothers and Menhaden*—which could trawl the deeper ocean waters for even more menhaden and return to the factory the same day, without the added inconvenience of the smaller liaison boats.

Things went well for the company until 1908, when the General Assembly outlawed menhaden fishing in Maryland for fear that too many edible fish were being harvested along with the inedible menhaden. Dennis immediately closed his Crisfield plant and reopened at a new facility in Dymer Creek, Virginia. In 1910, he moved the plant to yet another new facility at Sandy Point, near Cape Charles, Virginia. By 1917, however, political matters once again caught up with Dennis. The U.S. Navy confiscated his plant and turned it into a naval base, modifying its four steamboats as patrol vessels for the Eastern Shore coast. This seizure forced him to move operations back to Old Island, where he ran the former factory until closing in 1929. Fire consumed the building on July 21, 1932, leaving only the plant's brick chimney, which today remains a local landmark and navigation point for boats sailing into Crisfield.

Unlike oysters, terrapin and fish, not all marketable goods on the Chesapeake Bay in the late nineteenth century could be found underwater. Waterfowl, including ducks, geese and

In 1871, local businessmen L.E.P. Dennis and R.H. Mulligan established a menhaden-fertilizer factory on Old Island. Crews manned the company's large fishing schooners, hauling in menhaden by the thousands in the Chesapeake Bay and beyond. *Courtesy Scorchy Tawes.*

swan, were also plentiful in Somerset County and throughout the Eastern Shore. A staple of local diets through the mid-1800s, these birds saw high demand in many of the same markets as terrapin once rail travel made their mass export to inland cities possible.

Hunters sought to kill hundreds—sometimes up to a thousand—per week in season to sell to restaurants and markets in other parts of the country. Large skiffing guns could kill more than a hundred ducks with one shot, and the rise of affordable automatic shotguns in the early twentieth century allowed even the most amateur hunter to increase his catch. Waterfowl were shipped out of Somerset by the barrelful.

Like most of the rest of the Chesapeake Bay's bounties, however, these birds were overharvested. By the early 1920s, geese and swans in particular were becoming increasingly more difficult to find in large numbers. Maryland legislators passed laws in an attempt to preserve the population, but they had little effect. The decline of migratory waterfowl was a national problem. Eventually, the federal government stepped in to offer protection for certain wildfowl species. As with terrapin, their numbers have increased in the decades that have followed, but populations are nowhere near what they once were.

By the early 1900s, the oyster boom was turning into a bust. In 1912, the Maryland Shellfish Commission established a limit on the number of hours watermen could dredge and tong for oysters—fifty-eight days for dredgers, one hundred days for tongers. Storming the legislature in Annapolis, Eastern Shore watermen claimed such restrictions prevented them from earning a decent living.

Some even claimed those serving on the shellfish commission were merely puppets controlled by Maryland seafood packers, who wanted to keep oyster prices down. By then, wholesale prices had risen as high as one dollar per bushel. Throughout the twentieth century and into the twenty-first, local watermen fought an ongoing battle with the various regulatory agencies that oversaw their work on the bay, now combined as the Maryland Department of Natural Resources.

Within the next two years, Somerset's oyster industry fell to little more than a shadow of its former self. This is not to say either watermen or packers were giving up completely on oysters. In fact, an estimated sixty-thousand gallons—eighteen train cars' worth—of oysters were shipped from Crisfield on December 19, 1920. However, the years of the four-hundred-thousand-bushel catch were over.

The onset of World War I cut off the European oyster trade on which many of the local packers had come to rely. Increased competition from packers in Louisiana and Florida also forced many smaller seafood houses to scale back production or shut their doors entirely. Others turned their interests toward the emerging blue crab industry. With more boats registered in Crisfield by 1910 than any other port in the United States, local watermen had to have something to catch.

In 1903, Crisfield's hard crab catch was reported at 396,400 bushels, valued at about $300,000, and some 18 million soft crabs, valued around $400,000. On top of this, the city exported some fifty thousand gallons of canned crabmeat that year, worth about $1 per gallon.

That summer, about one hundred barrels of fish also were shipped from Crisfield each week via rail. Those barrels combined fetched as much as seven thousand dollars per week on the open market, predominately in New York and Philadelphia, as well as in Baltimore, where steamships made daily deliveries from Crisfield. Processors shipping from Crisfield included J.J. Tull and Co.; the Tangier Packing Co.; the A.P. Ford Co.; S.S. Coston; E.R. Lowe and Co.; Kelly, Noah and Co. and J.H. Riggin and Co.

That year, another seafood processor emerged as businessman John T. Handy opened a tomato and fish plant on Crisfield's waterfront. In 1917, the John T. Handy Co. began processing soft-shell crabs, as well, and an international industry was born. Today, Handy's Soft Shell Crabs are even more popular in Japan than they are in the United States.

Until the late 1800s, soft crabs were seen as little more than bait. However, one enterprising Crisfield waterman, Captain Tawes, began marketing them in Baltimore as a regional delicacy. By the early 1900s, they had become a cottage industry in Crisfield, growing exponentially from there. During the final week of August 1928, an estimated 1.5 million soft crabs were shipped from Crisfield by rail. That same week, packers in the city shipped some two hundred thousand hard crabs and twenty thousand gallons of picked crabmeat.

Boats of all types filled Crisfield Harbor in 1917. More boats were registered in Crisfield by 1910 than any other port in the United States.

Barrels of crabs like the ones in this 1930s photo were common in Crisfield during that decade as the seafood industry again boomed. Some 200,000 hard crabs were shipped from the city during the final week of August 1928 alone.

Small country stores like this one in Wenona served many of Somerset County's communities in the early 1900s. Economic prosperity brought on by the railroad and seafood industry allowed many storekeepers to make a comfortable living. *Courtesy Cindy Powell.*

Soon, Crisfield was recognized as the "Seafood Capital of the U.S.A." on a special indicia designed for the U.S. post office. By the 1940s, the city would call itself the "Seafood Capital of the World," a boast still used in many area marketing publications in the early twenty-first century, despite the fact that only a handful of seafood processors remain.

Though Crisfield once boasted more than one hundred operating seafood plants, only a few survived the turmoil that befell the industry throughout the twentieth century. One early prominent producer was George A. Christy. Working aboard dredge boats at a young age, Christy was paid one season with fifty dollars, a twelve-foot skiff and a pair of tongs. With this equipment, he set out on his own during the 1880 season, marketing his oysters as an independent watermen. The next year he married Elizabeth Sterling and put his new bride to work shucking the oysters he caught. They sold the shucked oysters to local stores by the quart and pint.

Prior to the 1882 season, Christy had $500 for a small sloop, allowing his small business to expand. He also hired others to help his wife shuck, allowing him to send a full barrel of oysters to market aboard the steamship to Baltimore most evenings. This operation allowed him to save enough money to purchase a full-fledged packing plant on the water at Tenth Street by 1890.

The business flourished. In 1910, Christy brought his son, Clarence, on as a partner in the business, naming it Geo. A. Christy and Son. It remained a family business—in later years under the guidance of Clarence's son, Richard—until its demise in the 1970s, nearly a century after George set out on his first solo oyster harvest. One element that allowed the company to operate so long while others failed was the Christy family's willingness to try new things. One of the more unique items the company once offered was "sea squab," a fancy name for the common swelling toad.

Like many of Crisfield's earliest oyster business, Christy's was located on Jersey Island, a section of marshland built up by oyster shells, not connected to the mainland. Early on, workers took a small ferry to the island, paying a penny per toll. In 1880, a drawbridge was constructed to allow pedestrians, horse carriages and, later, motor vehicles to reach the island. The Jersey Island Drawbridge was unique in that instead of raising and lowering, it actually rolled back upon itself to allow boats through.

Somerset County's coastal communities experienced a boom as the seafood industry took off. However, the rest of the county was not resting on its laurels. By the early twentieth century, nearly all of Somerset was a hotbed of commerce and newfound opportunities in education and recreation.

Chapter 8

Prosperity and Decline

While the seafood industry was booming in coastal areas of Somerset County, plans of a much different nature were coming to fruition inland at Princess Anne. Local ministers with the Delaware Conference of the Methodist Episcopal Church purchased sixteen acres of land to construct a new school, the Delaware Conference Academy. Opened on September 13, 1886, with one teacher and nine students, its enrollment grew to thirty-seven by the end of the year.

During the next three decades, it became known as Princess Anne Academy, serving as the industrial branch of Morgan State College. In 1919, Maryland officials operating the land grant program at the Caucasian-only Maryland Agricultural College at College Park sought a similar land grant program for African Americans. They took control of Princess Anne Academy for this purpose, renaming it Maryland Agricultural College Eastern Shore Branch. Full ownership of the former academy passed on to state officials in 1926. It became Maryland State College in 1948. Another name change, on October 1, 1970, gave the school its current moniker, University of Maryland Eastern Shore.

As Somerset's population expanded, education became increasingly important. On July 4, 1892, masons laid the cornerstone for a new school in Princess Anne, Washington Academy. Seen as the successor to Somerset Academy and even constructed from some of the brick salvaged from the old school building when it closed, it marked the beginning of modern public education in northern Somerset. Its early faculty consisted of Luther Martin, who served as Maryland's attorney general, and Hugh Breckenridge, who went on to become the chief justice of Pennsylvania.

About a decade later, Somerset also outgrew its old courthouse. The current version, considered a Somerset landmark today, was constructed in 1904, offering more room for the judicial process and more importantly, social gatherings. It also put an end to ventilation problems the former courthouse had suffered for more than seventy years.

Back in Crisfield, more recreational opportunities were created. In 1892, a chapter of the International Order of Odd Fellows was initiated in the city, quickly becoming one of the area's most popular fraternal organizations. An ornate Odd Fellows Hall—later called the Crisfield Opera House—was built at the corner of Main and Fourth Streets. The Odd Fellows remained in Crisfield until financial struggles led to their demise in 1929.

Maryland State College, seen here in the 1960s, became the University of Maryland Eastern Shore in 1970.

Meanwhile a second fraternal organization, one native to Crisfield, was formed in the oyster house of Wesley Milligan, near the steamboat wharf. Called Slaz Fleet, it was perhaps the bawdiest club of its kind ever to exist in Somerset County. Initiation into Slaz Fleet consisted of three activities performed by every new member. In the first, the inductee had to reach the top of a greased pole. In the second, the initiated member was lowered into a barrel and continuously rolled over the oyster house's rough planks. The third saw the new member placed into an oyster bin, filled with obstacles made of discarded oystering tools, where he would be expected to wrestle with a club member dressed as Satan for five minutes or until the new inductee yelled the mercy call "sacco," whichever came first.

Slaz Fleet was unique in that its meetings were held at nine o'clock in the evening to allow even the busiest businessman to join. Fines were levied for any member who missed a meeting, and the treasury was spent predominately on beer, whisky and cigars, which usually ensured well-attended meetings in the first place. Said to have been comprised of nearly every grown man in Crisfield at the time, Slaz Fleet did have its charitable side, as well. Its members were expected to attend church dinners and similar festivals en masse, ensuring high profits at such events.

Still, it was the church that ultimately did in Slaz Fleet. In less than two years, the organization was disbanded when it was condemned by the area's religious leaders, as well as many of the members' wives.

Students gathered in front of old Washington Academy during this 1930s scene. The building's cornerstone was laid July 4, 1892.

Seen here in 1997, the current Somerset County Courthouse was built in 1904.

Many former Slaz Fleet members moved their membership to the tamer (though not by much tamer, by some accounts) Odd Fellows. Others found their niche in athletics. Crisfield's first organized baseball team was formed in 1892 to compete against other teams throughout the Delmarva Peninsula, which later included Smith Island. Baseball reigned supreme in Crisfield and throughout much of the Eastern Shore until the late 1940s.

Granted, some also found less constructive ways to amuse themselves. According to the July 20, 1901 edition of the Cambridge-based *Democrat and News*:

> *While one hears of persons being struck by lightning every day, it is quite consoling to know there is a man in Crisfield who wanted to be struck by lightning to such an extent that he affixed a lightning rod to his head and ran about the fields during an electrical storm. While passing beneath a tree, it was struck by a bolt of lightning, and the man was felled to the ground by a large splinter. We are not informed if this was a good enough substitute or whether he wanted a perfect realization.*

Anchored by the success of the seafood industry, the early 1900s brought about many new businesses and small industries in Somerset County. By 1903, Crisfield boasted three garment factories: the Asbury Shirt Manufacturing Co., Baptist Shirt Co. and Crisfield Shirt Factory. The city even had two competing ice cream manufacturers: the Crisfield Ice Cream Co. and Sterling Ice Cream Works.

Many of these early twentieth-century businesses were more intertwined with the seafood industry itself. The Crisfield Ice Manufacturing Co., for example, produced and stored ice to keep seafood cool in the day's unrefrigerated railcars. Entrepreneur W.H. Norwood made sails so workboats could travel out and harvest the seafood in the first place. The Potomac Poultry Food Co. built a large shell crushing plant on Crisfield's waterfront to take advantage of the natural byproducts of oyster shucking. Later, the plant produced lime fertilizer from the crushed shells. However, perhaps the one entrepreneur who made the most out of Somerset County's seafood industry without once commercially harvesting an oyster was Charles D. Briddell.

Born in Marumsco in 1882, Briddell showed a passion for metalworking early on when he began creating penknives from scrap metal at about age ten. Upon learning he could make money from his creations by selling them to his classmates for a dime each, an industry was born. Briddell's father, David, removed him from school in the fifth grade and encouraged him to focus on honing his natural abilities. Using makeshift tools, he established a small shop in an old carriage house on his family's farm, creating and repairing small farm implements for neighbors.

Visits to Crisfield with his father usually meant a stop at James Loreman's blacksmith shop near what is now Main and Ninth Streets, where Briddell would learn by watching Loreman perform his daily tasks. Briddell usually bought a few cents' worth of iron from Loreman to take back to Marumsco and practice creating hooks and chain links. By age fifteen, he had expanded into the manufacture of oyster tongs, which he sometimes would deliver himself on his bicycle. Outgrowing the carriage house, he built a new workshop using timber from the family farm. There, he became proficient in horseshoeing and taught himself to build wagon and cart bodies to add to his profits when the metalworking business was light.

By his marriage to Grace Mae Maddox in 1905, he was enjoying a rising reputation throughout Somerset County. In 1906 he moved his business to Marion Station. However, building his first shop off the farm proved financially risky, and he soon found both his home and business mortgaged. However, he continued to rent the Marion facility and, dropping his carriage-making business, returned his focus to metalworking full-time. Still, hardship continued. Fire destroyed the shop before the year's end.

Briddell remained undeterred, reopening the day after the fire in an abandoned building with basic tools borrowed from other area blacksmiths. By 1910, he had moved beyond simple blacksmithing to experimentation with metal tempering processes. Through these experiments, he developed the Briddell oyster knife, an implement with a stronger blade than any other on the market. The tool became such an industry standard that the City of Crisfield still incorporates it—along with the Briddell crab knife—into its design of the keys to the city.

In 1914, Briddell moved his enterprise to a building on the corner of Ninth and Main Streets in Crisfield, where his workshop and early plant expanded into an large operation, exporting oyster knives and other implements to every state on the East Coast, as well as some countries in South America. By 1920, business had grown so much that it was time to expand again. He moved into yet another new building on Crisfield's Main Street.

Five years later he took another giant step forward in the business world, incorporating his plant. A line of ice tools was added, and the ease of rail shipments turned them into a national success. Charles D. Briddell Inc. was well on its way to becoming the largest single employer in Crisfield. Even as the Great Depression struck, Briddell rose above the nation's woes, continuing production and providing jobs for many and reaching into his own pocket to help those out of work when his work force was full.

By 1936, Briddell had helped Crisfield get back on its feet. He operated three plants in the downtown area by then, and orders were booming. The local economy was stronger than that in other areas of the county thanks to the numbers he employed. Two years later, on August 31, 1938, he tiredly announced he was leaving work early to go home and rest. Before midnight he had passed away. However, the company he founded continued to thrive until the late 1990s.

Blacksmiths like Briddell became increasingly important in Somerset County throughout the early 1900s, not only for the seafood industry, but also for the agriculture industry. By the 1880s, strawberries had become a popular crop in Somerset localities including Marion Station and Westover. In the early 1900s, they practically took over Marion, with almost all available land cleared to make way for berry crops, earning the small town the stately nickname "Strawberry Capital of the World."

Like the seafood boom in coastal areas, the strawberry boom in Marion provided employment for many and made hundreds of thousands of dollars for farmers throughout the county. While seafood houses in Crisfield paid their oyster shuckers in

The workers on Paul Gunby's farm in this 1920s photo exemplified one of the most common careers in Marion Station. The fruit was planted in nearly every field throughout the town, earning it the nickname "Strawberry Capital of the World."

Marion Station's strawberry auction block drew buyers from as far away as Chicago, paying a record thirty cents per quart by 1918.

redeemable tokens, strawberry farmers paid their pickers with tickets, also known as checks or coupons. These heavy cardboard tickets were preprinted with the name of the farmer and the number of quarts picked. At the end of the week, strawberry ticket holders would turn in their tickets in exchange for payment of that week's picking rate, which fluctuated with the market. Those who could not wait did have other options, however. The branch of the American grocery store chain once located in Marion was known to have accepted strawberry tickets in lieu of monetary payment in some cases.

By 1918, strawberry sales in Marion had reached an all-time high of thirty cents per quart. Buyers from as far away as Chicago would come to the auction block established in Marion to purchase strawberries in bulk for grocery stores and other retail establishments. However, the berry's glory days were headed to an end. By the early 1920s, Marion's nutrient-drained soil was yielding fewer strawberries each year.

The Great Depression hurt local farmers even more, as strawberries became a luxury item rather than a necessity for many merchants who once flocked to the strawberry auction. Growers began selling their land for whatever they could get, which often was not much. Berry prices dropped below a nickel per quart. By the onset of World War II, the strawberry boom was a distant memory in Somerset County.

Through national sales, local strawberry farmers made their mark on agriculture in the United States. However, by far the Somerset County resident who had the most impact on American agriculture was John Wesley Nelson. Born near Crisfield on October 3, 1853, Nelson was part of a poor family. As a teenager, he struck out on his own in Baltimore, eventually making his way to Chicago, where he worked for his uncle, Riley McCready. While work there was steady, Nelson could not help but think a greater reward awaited him elsewhere, in the wilds of California.

Working his way west as a peddler, he arrived in San Francisco disillusioned that no more opportunities presented themselves there than they had in Chicago or Baltimore. He hiked up the Oregon Trail to find even less luck in Oregon. Returning to California, he found a job with a small fruit grower. A short time later, he was promoted to foreman.

Eventually he bought the company, transforming it into the California Packing Corporation. In 1916, he trademarked a new name for the company's highest-quality line of canned fruits: Del Monte. Products packaged under the Del Monte brand earned a vast following throughout the nation, allowing Nelson to amass a great fortune upon selling the company in the 1920s. It continues today under the trade name Del Monte Foods.

While Nelson was busy building an empire in California, his home county continued to grow. Marion Academy, the first public school in Marion Station, was built in the late 1800s.

A new school, Marion Central School, replaced it in 1912, the same year Somerset saw its first Boy Scouts of America troop, in Crisfield. The county's first hospital, Somerset Hospital, opened in Marion in 1908. Crisfield High School was founded to replace the former Crisfield Academy that same year. From 1898 to 1919, the Oriole Telephone Co. served residents in its service area before being absorbed by the Chesapeake and Potomac Telephone Co.

As strawberries boomed, so did commerce in downtown Marion Station, evidenced by this 1930s photo. By the onset of World War II, however, the berry's heyday was a distant memory in Somerset County.

The first public schoolhouse on Smith Island also was opened in the late 1800s. *Island Belle*, the venerable mail boat between Crisfield and Smith Island, began service in the 1910s, emulating a similar service that existed between Crisfield and Tangier Island, Virginia. Communities thriving on Smith Island included Tylerton, Ewell, Rhodes Point and Long Branch, the latter having since disappeared as an island settlement.

However, that is not to say all was well in Somerset in the early 1900s. On New Year's Day 1910, the Tangier mail boat *Orine* was sunk off the coast of Crisfield in a storm. Nearly six weeks later, on February 12, a fire at the Baltimore, Chesapeake and Atlantic Railway Co. warehouse burned the Crisfield steamboat wharf, killing night watchman J. Dallas Collins.

The fire also destroyed thousands of dollars' worth of freight, including pianos, furniture, boat engines and barrels of oysters and clams. Collins's body later was found under the docks, leading many to suspect foul play was involved. That May, tragedy struck the area again as the roof of Immanuel Methodist Episcopal Church, under construction on Crisfield's Main Street, collapsed, killing contractor Charles Matthews and injuring two others.

Then there was the alcohol problem. In November 1910, nationally famous temperance advocate and saloon smasher Carrie Nation came to Crisfield, where a local option law had banned alcohol, but gave rise to a large number of speakeasies. While Nation did not attack the city's known liquor dispensers (she saved that for the next week, when she destroyed a pool hall in Parksley, Virginia, rumored to be a speakeasy), she did take time to offer a lecture on the dangers of alcohol at Crisfield's Lyric Theater.

Marion Central School, seen here under construction, opened to students in 1912.

This early view of Oriole's Main Street shows what the town looked like during the days of the Oriole Telephone Co., in operation from 1898 to 1919.

Mail, school and other service boats founded in the early 1900s remain a staple of island life in the early twenty-first century. From left are service boats *Island Belle*, *Miss Whitelock* and *Island Star* at Smith Island in the 1960s.

Bootleg liquor continued to be a problem in Crisfield even with the passage of the Volstead Act of 1919, which gave rise to prohibition throughout the United States. According to a November 1925 article sent to the *Baltimore News* by Crisfield correspondent F.D. Sears, many locals claimed the Volstead Act made bootlegging even worse in the area, attributing a rash of burglaries to those seeking money for illegal alcohol. Indeed, easy access to Crisfield, Smith Island, Deal Island and other coastal areas by both land and water made Somerset County a hotbed for bootleggers during prohibition.

In 1911, the *Crisfield Times*, established in 1889 as the city's principal paper, ran an editorial depicting the area as it may have been seen through the eyes of a visitor. The description of Crisfield included "poles to the right, left, in front and behind one; besides they were all types, grades, sizes and shapes, with wires strung in any and every conceivable way. Furthermore, there were fireflies hung on certain poles, which I was afterward told was the way in which this town received its street lighting" and "brick, cement, ashes, wood and dirt walks of every shape and every height, in repair and out of repair—you take your pick."

It was clear the area was still rough around the edges. A 1912 fire in the city's Jersey Island section that caused a brief slump in the seafood packing industry did not help matters. Still, growth continued. Somerset's first U.S. Army National Guard unit was founded in 1914 with Company L, third battalion of the 115th Infantry Regiment, 29th Division, was organized in Crisfield. Under the leadership of Captain Hiram Collins,

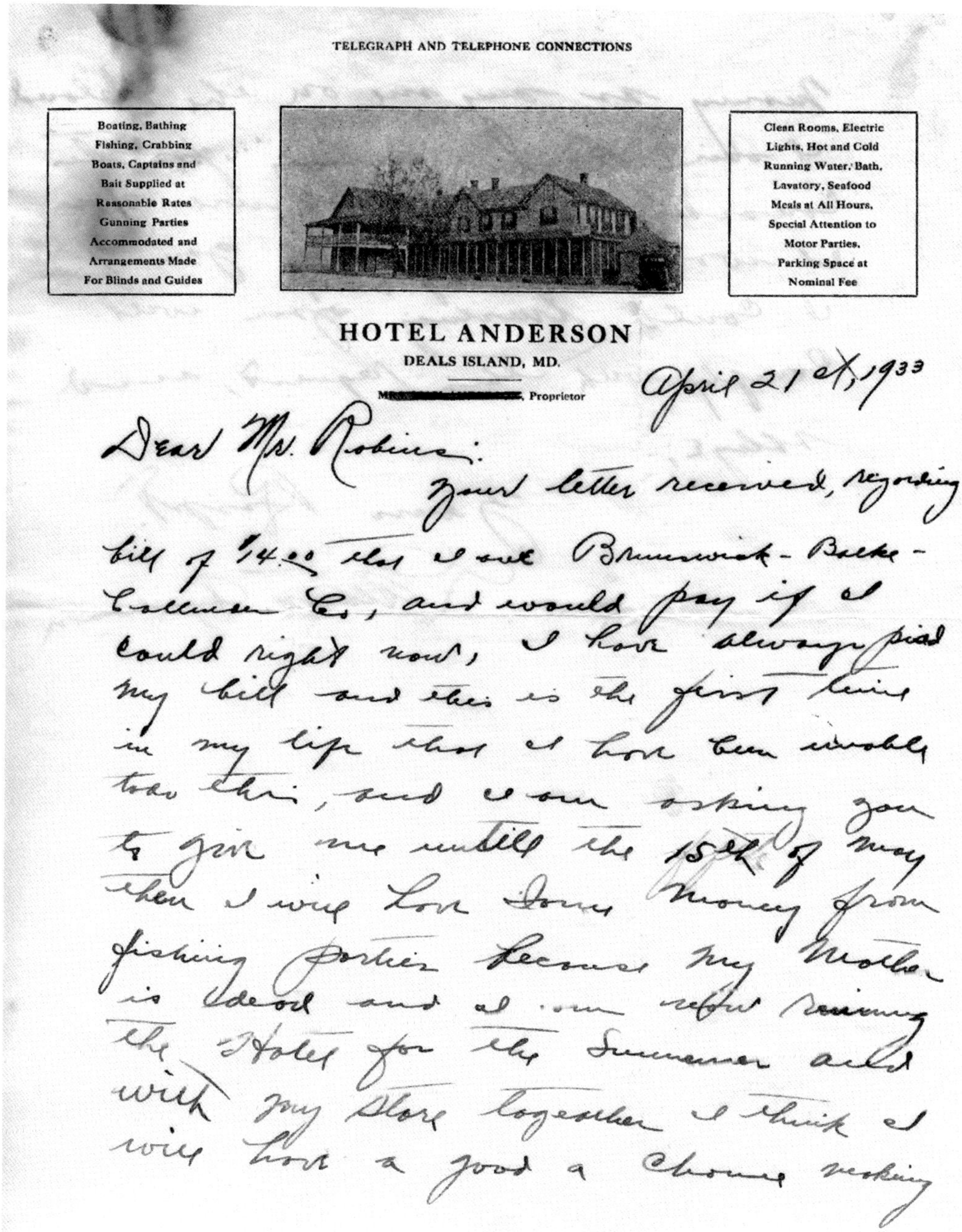

TELEGRAPH AND TELEPHONE CONNECTIONS

Boating, Bathing
Fishing, Crabbing
Boats, Captains and
Bait Supplied at
Reasonable Rates
Gunning Parties
Accommodated and
Arrangements Made
For Blinds and Guides

Clean Rooms, Electric
Lights, Hot and Cold
Running Water, Bath,
Lavatory, Seafood
Meals at All Hours,
Special Attention to
Motor Parties,
Parking Space at
Nominal Fee

HOTEL ANDERSON

DEALS ISLAND, MD.

[redacted], Proprietor

April 21st, 1933

Dear Mr. Robins:

Your letter received, regarding bill of $14.00 that I owe Brunswick-Balke-Collender Co, and would pay if I could right now, I have always paid my bill and this is the first time in my life that I have been unable todo this, and I am asking you to give me untill the 15th of May then I will have some money from fishing parties because my Mother is dead and I am after running the Hotel for the Summer and with my Store together I think I will have a good a chance making

The Anderson Hotel was Deal Island's major landmark during the prohibition era, though it had little to do with bootlegging. The business offered electric lights, hot water and seafood dinners. Parking for motor vehicles costed extra.

the unit was sent to guard the Mexican-American border before being deployed overseas in 1918 to help defend France during World War I.

On the homefront, Somerset residents received a glimpse at the dangers they may have faced as the U.S. Navy battleship *North Dakota* anchored in Crisfield Harbor in February 1917 to guard local ports against possible German attacks. However, the ship was viewed more as a curiosity than a harbinger of war in Somerset or anywhere else on U.S. soil. In fact, World War I proved good for the local economy. In June 1917, sailmaker Charles Richardson received a contract to make tents for the U.S. Army. The agreement allowed him to hire fifty employees to meet the demand.

In 1919, the sixteenth American Legion post in Maryland was founded in Crisfield, named in remembrance of fallen Crisfield soldier Stanley Cochrane. The state's ninety-fourth post, named in remembrance of soldier Oliver Beauchamp Jr., was later established in Princess Anne.

The first members of the Crisfield post sought a way to memorialize their fallen comrades, and they found one in the way of a $2,500 statue, *Spirit of the American Doughboy*, produced from a popular design by Indiana sculptor Ernest Moore Viquesney. Unveiled at Crisfield Veterans Cemetery on Decoration Day 1922, a plaque on the statue's granite base was inscribed with the names of the nine Crisfield residents killed in the line of duty during World War I. In all, twenty-six Somerset residents are known to have perished in the war.

Meanwhile, locals continued to find new ways to entertain themselves. In the early 1900s, Somerset County saw its first amusement park, Hastings Electric Park, near the current site of the Maurice D. Tawes Armory on Main Street Extended in Crisfield. Its attractions included a merry-go-round, a Ferris wheel, swings, a shooting gallery, an "Ocean Wave" ride and a roller skating rink. By 1919 its name had changed to Central Park, a moniker it kept until its closing in the 1920s.

Two more amusement parks followed in Crisfield. Asbury Park, in the Down Neck district near Crisfield, opened in 1915. It featured, among other things, a carousel, a monkey show and the Palace Auditorium, a combination concert hall and roller skating rink. Bay Ridge Park, operated in the vicinity of the area of Crisfield now known as LaVallettes, was opened in the 1920s by Lorie C. Quinn Jr., but went bankrupt in 1931. Its amusements included a carousel, Ferris wheel, lighted swimming pool, bowling alleys and seaplane rides. The land on which this park once sat has since eroded.

Movies also had become a favorite pastime for many Somerset residents. While formal theaters, like the Lyric in Crisfield, existed, many movie houses existed throughout the county in the form of projections onto bare walls, sheets and anything else that could constitute a movie screen in old barns, empty warehouses and even on the sides of buildings. In a 2004 letter to the *Crisfield Times*, former resident Margaret Pasquella remembered what might have been the first such theater in lower Somerset:

> *In my early teens, I was thrilled with the silent movies. My father* [George "Pony" Lawson] *opened the first movie house on the second floor of his shirt factory on Asbury*

Unveiled at Crisfield Veterans Cemetery on Decoration Day 1922, a plaque on the *Spirit of the American Doughboy*'s granite base was inscribed with the names of the nine Crisfield residents killed in the line of duty during World War I.

> *Avenue* [in Crisfield]. *One funny story he would like to tell is when a scene in a movie showed the main characters in a driving rainstorm, one old Down Necker left abruptly with his wife because he had forgotten "to shut up the chickens." Unfortunately, the screen had to be replaced once when another moviegoer brought his shotgun and shot the villain.*

While most Somerset natives were still getting used to watching motion pictures, one was starring in them. Born March 6, 1882, Lilyan Stratton Corbin was the daughter of Alex and Henrietta Corbin. A Civil War veteran, her father worked at L.E.P. Dennis and Son. The family was impoverished, living in shack on Old Island. Mr. Corbin saved his meager wages from the factory and eventually managed to buy a small house in Crisfield near Ward's Crossing. Shortly thereafter, he and Henrietta separated, then divorced.

As her parents moved and remarried, Lilyan found herself with a very extended family. As was the custom with many children at the time, she also found herself without a formal education, something public school officials sought to rectify when, at age fourteen, she was placed in the first grade and assigned a six-year-old tutor. This did not sit well with the teenager. Inside of a year she quit school and sought a better life by running away via train to New York. With no money in her pockets, she got a job selling newspapers, making a penny's profit per paper.

It was through this endeavor that she met a gentleman named Mayall, a Wall Street banker who took her under his wing and taught her about the finer things in life, not the least of which were reading and writing. Upon his death in 1904, he left his fortune to Ms. Corbin, making her a relatively rich woman at the turn of the century. It was the age of silent films, and the Crisfield native had her heart set on becoming an actress. In 1905 she married actor Frank Campeau and went on to secure small parts in his and other movies. For many of these parts she took on the stage name "Lilyan Stratton," a name that would stay with her the rest of her life.

Achieving modest success in early silent movies, Corbin returned to Somerset County from New York, purchasing a home in Westover. She often divided her time between there and an estate she had bought in New Jersey. In 1917, she and Campeau were divorced. Shortly thereafter she married a Dutch immigrant who had come to America following World War I. Together, they invested Corbin's fortune and saw it return many times over.

She became a philanthropist in her hometown, loaning money with no guarantee of payment, seeking out those who lived in poverty as she once had and offering financial assistance. She offered numerous scholarships to allow students to complete high school and even college so they could have the educational benefits she never had. During this time she expanded her resume, authoring four novels: *Reno* (named for the Las Vegas city in which she and Campeau were divorced), *Homing*, *The Feminine Philosophy* and *The Wife's Lesson*.

While Corbin was an avid supporter of Somerset and its people, she was not to spend her last moments in the county. While driving with her niece, Blance Hurst, in Parsippany, New Jersey, on November 1, 1928, Corbin's scarf flew over her face, covering her eyes and causing her to swerve off the road. The crash ended her life. A mausoleum built for Lilyan Corbin's ashes at the site of the current Carter G. Woodson Elementary School was a target for vandalism. Many believed incorrectly that she had been buried with her riches.

Following Corbin's death, her husband announced he would use part of the family's fortune to build a library to benefit all people of Crisfield. Upon that library's completion on Main Street Extended in 1930, the urn containing Corbin's ashes was moved to the new building, where it remains today.

In 1919, yet another automobile accident led to the establishment of another of Somerset County's long-standing institutions, Edward W. McCready Memorial Hospital in Crisfield. On September 13, wealthy Chicago cork magnate Edward W. McCready was driving from the home of his stepmother, Susie McCready, in Crisfield, to meet his wife, Caroline, in Atlantic City, New Jersey, when he misjudged the distance of a train coming through Westover. McCready's car was about midway into a railroad crossing when it was struck by the morning passenger train, on its way to Crisfield.

McCready and one of his passengers, his daughter Sue Anne's nurse, Margaret Steinback, were killed instantly. The other passenger, Sue Anne, lived briefly and was transported to the Crisfield General and Marine Hospital. Founded in 1910 as Somerset County's second hospital, the facility was said to have been one of the best in the region, but its cramped quarters left little to be desired. Following the closing of Somerset Hospital in 1917, it became the county's only large-scale medical facility. A flu epidemic that year filled its meager rooms and halls to overflowing.

Caroline McCready was summoned from New Jersey, but arrived too late. The doctors were unable to save her daughter. Furthermore, Crisfield scarcely had many of the amenities she was used to in Chicago. Even the local funeral homes did not have the facilities to keep her husband and daughter's bodies until funeral arrangements could be made. Hospital superintendent Florence Smith offered to store the bodies in the facility's reception room until they could be transported to Philadelphia, where they would be cremated for interment in Chicago. She also offered Mrs. McCready a room at the hospital during her time in Crisfield, refusing to charge the widow for any services rendered.

Touched by Smith's kindness, McCready met with directors of the General and Marine Hospital, informing them she intended to build a much larger, state-of-the-art facility for Crisfield and Somerset County. She kept her promise, opening the new $200,000 hospital in her husband's memory on the Annemessex River at Cork Point, former home of the McCready family, on May 6, 1923. Early rates were $2 per day for a ward and $7 per day for a private room. Operations were disallowed in the evenings and on Sundays.

Two months after the hospital's opening, Somerset County gained statewide attention for a much different but no less important event: the discovery of the will of Charles Lord Calvert I, the third Lord of Baltimore, in records at the Somerset County Courthouse in Princess Anne. Likely not seen since Calvert's death in 1714, the will became an important historical document in Maryland.

The urn containing the ashes of Liilyan Stratton Corbin was moved to the library named in her honor upon its completion in 1930.

Edward W. McCready Memorial Hospital, seen here in the 1940s, was a gift from Caroline McCready in honor of the concern shown for her at the former Crisfield General and Marine Hospital upon the death of her husband and daughter.

Of more interest to many in Somerset County at that time was the Eastern Shore League, a professional Class D baseball league formed in 1922 with teams in Crisfield; Salisbury; Pocomoke City; Cambridge; Laurel, Delaware; and Parksley, Virginia. Crisfield won only one pennant during the six years the league existed, but they made it count. During their championship season in 1926, the Crisfield Crabbers (also the name of the high school team) posted a winning percentage of .750, setting a professional baseball record.

In the 1930s and 1940s, Crisfield's community teams would go on to participate in other shore leagues. Throughout the first half of the twentieth century, the city's community teams also competed against other community teams, including those on Smith Island.

However, fortunes were about to take a dive in the southern Somerset City. On March 29, 1928, less than a year after the breakup of the Eastern Shore League, the face of Crisfield's downtown area changed dramatically thanks to what is known today as the Great Fire of 1928. Patrons were watching the Greta Garbo movie *Love* at the Arcade Theater in the Crisfield Opera House that evening when news of a fire in the projection room reached the audience, which was leisurely evacuated.

In less than an hour, those who had gathered to watch the building burn were much more panicked as brisk winds fanned the flames. Buildings quickly caught fire one by one, the blaze leaving little but charred shells in its wake. Soon telephone, telegraph and electrical service to the entire city was down due to the fiery destruction of communication and electrical lines. Water service also ceased, as there was no electricity to power the pumps at the municipal water plant.

Designated community members drove eighteen miles to Westover to telephone for assistance from surrounding areas as the Crisfield Volunteer Fire Department attempted to control the blaze. Firemen from Princess Anne, Pocomoke City, Salisbury and Delmar in Maryland, and Seaford and Laurel in Delaware, responded to the cry for help. With six fire departments pumping water continuously, the standpipe, which replaced the windmill at Kennerly's Wharf as the city's main water supply in 1898, was quickly drained. A pumping engine was quickly dispatched to the area now occupied by Somers Cove Marina to pull up water and provide it to other engines fighting the fire.

By the time the fire was contained, it had swept its way to Pine Street, decimating the Pennsylvania Railroad station there. In all, nearly $1 million in damage was reported. Ninety buildings disappeared virtually overnight, more than three hundred were forced out of work immediately and sixty-six lost their homes. Yet only one casualty was recorded. Frank Morgan, a child from Crisfield, died from injuries sustained from the collapse of a building wall.

Suffering their third—and largest—great fire since 1910, Crisfield's leaders remained optimistic. Business owners reopened within days in temporary tin shacks erected where their buildings once stood. City officials adopted a new slogan, "Build for the future," and encouraged those rebuilding their stores to use fireproof materials including brick and concrete.

Only burned shells of buildings remained on most of Crisfield's Main Street following the Great Fire of 1928.

Following the Great Fire, merchants hastily constructed inexpensive tin shacks from which they conducted business until permanent buildings could be reconstructed along Main Street.

The residents of Marion Station also suffered their share of fires in the 1920s, many at the hands of the "Fire Bug of Marion." In 1924, a man later identified as Warfield Townsend, given the "Fire Bug" nickname by local newspapers, burned many of the town's most prominent structures, starting with its railroad station. Though fires at the station were discovered before they caused much damage, he continued his path of destruction at other buildings, including Marion Central School and several private homes. A fire he set at Trinity Methodist Protestant Church destroyed the structure. The Central School fire led to the construction of Marion High School that same year.

Townsend took his vendetta against the railroad to an even greater extreme, attempting on three occasions to derail the passenger train from Princess Anne to Crisfield, twice by placing large equipment on the tracks and once by opening a switch track. Railroad officials discovered the obstructions in all three instances before any damage was done. In February 1925, the Maryland Lunacy Commission declared Townsend insane and committed him to an institution. After a decade of confinement, he was released in 1935 and lived an otherwise uneventful life in the Fruitland area of Wicomico County until his death in 1963.

Marion Station experienced another terrifying thrill on March 2, 1934, when a U.S. mail plane crash-landed at the Carl C. Green dairy farm near the town en route from Newark, New Jersey, to Richmond, Virginia. U.S. Army Lieutenant Harold Dietz, the plane's pilot, reportedly dipped the craft too low, losing control of the plane when it brushed some pine trees. Dietz was taken to McCready Memorial Hospital, where he made a full recovery after suffering a fractured skull and other injuries. He died four years later during a crash at an air show in his hometown of Easton, Pennsylvania.

At the time of Dietz's crash, Somerset was still reeling from an encounter several months before that had effects so far-reaching it made the pages of *Time* magazine. In October 1933, Mary Denston, an elderly resident of Kingston, was attacked by a man while walking down the road. Lieutenant Salisbury of the Maryland State Police later arrested George Armwood, a twenty-four-year-old African American, for the crime. Armwood was transported to Baltimore, where he signed a confession, and then was ordered back to the county jail in Princess Anne.

A mob formed at the jail with Armwood inside. At least one person likened the prisoner to Euel Lee, an African American who, at the conclusion of a controversial trial ending just the week before, was found guilty of murdering a family in neighboring Worcester County in 1931. Twenty-two police officers guarded the jail. Local troops refused orders from Governor Albert Ritchie to assist them. The mob stormed the jail, knocking down thirteen of the officers on guard and battering down the door.

The portion of the mob that was able to enter the jail beat Armwood senseless, then dragged him out bleeding from the head and chest so the rest of the crowd could have at him. A young boy reportedly jumped on his back and cut off his ear. Armwood was unconscious by then and dead by the time the mob hung his lifeless body from an oak tree in sight of the home of Robert Duer, Somerset County judge. Dangling from the tree, his clothes were set ablaze. His body was then dragged back to the county courthouse, covered in gasoline and lit afire again.

Once the crowd dispersed, state troopers claimed Armstrong's remains. The rope used in the lynching was cut into pieces and taken as souvenirs by several in attendance, including Denston's son, William, a police officer in Lower Merion Township, Pennsylvania.

The incident ignited national outrage. Many Maryland residents on the Western Shore called for Ritchie's resignation, saying he should have done more to prevent vigilantism in the county. Ritchie, meanwhile, blamed Duer and John Robins, state's attorney for Somerset County, for ordering Armwood's return to Princess Anne in the first place. The governor launched an investigation, but it did not get very far. Somerset Sheriff Luther Daugherty said he was at the lynching, but did not recognize a single face in the mob. They all must have been from Virginia, he surmised. He was voted out of office the next year.

Another death in Somerset County three years later—accidental this time—made statewide if not national headlines. In late January of 1936, the Chesapeake Bay froze solid. On February 1, residents looking in the right direction may have spied the third airship ever to fly over the area—the *Graf* zeppelin had flown over on October 15, 1928, followed by the U.S. Navy airship *Akron* during a reconnaissance mission in November 1931—as a Goodyear blimp sailed over Tangier Island, Virginia, to determine if its residents needed food or medical treatment.

The frozen bay had prohibited water travel to either Tangier or Smith Island and cut off all communications to or from the mainland. Though both islands were fully stocked for the winter, save for some medication that was needed, airplanes were brought in to deliver food, fuel and other supplies. The Somerset County chapter of the American Red Cross also sent nurses.

Of more concern were the island watermen who had been plying the waters of Tangier Sound when the freeze-up struck. By February 4, about 125 of them walked across the ice to Crisfield, where they were housed at the National Guard armory. That same day two men, Albert Rich and Pete Gray, attempted to test the durability of the ice by riding a motorcycle across it. The vehicle broke through and sank, its riders returning to the mainland on foot.

On February 5, about one hundred of the island watermen stranded in Crisfield formed a mass exodus back across the ice to the U.S. Coast Guard cutter *Travis*, which was attempting to break ice about three miles out in Tangier Sound. The men held onto long ropes so if one of them fell through a thin patch of ice, the others could easily pull them out. Once they reached *Travis*, the ship would ferry them across the portion of the sound it had broken up already, allowing them to disembark onto the thicker ice on the other side and walk back to their respective islands.

Most of those men were asleep at home in their own beds when the situation took a turn for the worst. On February 6, a storm that would become the worst blizzard of the twentieth century in Somerset County blew in. From Princess Anne to Crisfield, snow covered every available surface. Drifts rose up to ten feet high. Overland travel

Sargeant Wilbert Hunter stood in Crisfield just hours before his death during an expedition to Tangier Island on February 7, 1936.

was out of the question for the average citizen. Those who did manage to get out on foot reportedly did so only out of desperation when they ran out of coal for heat. They would return carrying as much as they could in sacks.

In the midst of the blizzard, Governor Harry Nice sent Major Enoch Garey, superintendent of the Maryland State Police, and his assistant, Sergeant Wilbert Hunter, to Crisfield to arrange assistance for the islands.

Organizing an expedition of about fifteen volunteers, mostly from Crisfield, and a small cache of newspaper reporters and photographers, Garey and Hunter set out across the frozen sound as the storm still raged, around dusk on February 7. They had planned a route across the ice from LaVallettes to *Travis*. They carried with them two large sleds full of food and supplies, planning to deliver them to Tangier Island the same way the watermen had returned home two days earlier.

On the fourth hour of the journey, tragedy struck: Hunter broke through the ice. Though he was able to scramble out of the frigid waters, the weather proved too much. By the time the expedition reached *Travis* three hours later, he was dead. Making matters worse, *Travis* wasn't going anywhere. Stuck in the very ice it was attempting to break, a second cutter, *Apache*, was dispatched to free the ship.

Two days later, a state tugboat arrived to retrieve Hunter's body and deliver it to Norfolk, Virginia, the closest port not frozen in. He was buried in his hometown of Parkville, Maryland, on February 12.

From February 18 to February 20, a board of inquiry based at the Crisfield Armory attempted to resolve the issue and clarify the events that led to Hunter's death. The public had crucified Garey's reputation; however, no official action was taken against him, despite testimony that several local residents had advised him against the maneuver. Questions also arose as to why the Maryland State Police were offering aid to Tangier in lieu of Smith Island without a request or input from Virginia authorities. Alas, those questions remained unanswered.

Happier times were on the horizon. In 1939, a young boy named Charlie Adams worked his first day selling copies of the *Crisfield Times* at the corner of Ninth and Main Streets in Crisfield. Throughout the years, Adams would become a Somerset County institution in himself, seldom missing a week of work selling newspapers until his retirement on December 20, 2006. By then his usual sales spot had been recognized by Crisfield officials for more than a decade as Charlie Adams Corner, complete with its own street sign.

While Adams's retirement was met with great fanfare, it likely did not compare to the scene on Main Street in 1938 when residents turned out in force to meet the president of the United States. Throughout the years, several U.S. presidents have visited Somerset County, though most of their tours have been unannounced. Woodrow Wilson reportedly visited in 1913, making an unpublicized visit to Make Peace. Calvin Coolidge came to the area during his presidency, stopping to worship at Immanuel Church in Crisfield. An Associated Press photographer snapped a picture of Herbert Hoover fishing off the coast of Crisfield in 1932. Hoover reportedly caught fifteen trout, one of them three feet long.

Members of the 1936 expedition to Tangier Island posed aboard and in front of the U.S. Coast Guard cutter *Travis*, demonstrating how thick the ice had become on the surface of Tangier Sound.

Posed at his namesake corner in the early 1990s, *Crisfield Times* paper carrier Charlie Adams was a fixture at Ninth and Main Streets from 1939 until his retirement in 2006.

Even Franklin D. Roosevelt visited, unannounced, in 1934, during a tour of the Eastern Shore aboard the U.S. Commerce Department boat *Sequoia*. The president began his tour in Crisfield, where vehicles from Washington, D.C., met the president and his small party. The group toured Make Peace before heading up the road to Pocomoke City, where it caused quite a stir. The president, it seems, had a craving for a good cigar and a bottle of Coca-Cola, and an establishment on Pocomoke's Market Street footed the bill nicely.

The brief stop provided enough time for word to spread and a smattering of Pocomoke residents to turn out and see President Roosevelt before he headed off to tour Beverly Mansion. From there, he ventured to All Hallows Episcopal Church in Snow Hill before returning to Crisfield, where word had spread of his arrival. While the streets were not mobbed, the president found it obligatory to tip his hat to a few good people on his way back to *Sequoia*, on which he sailed back to Washington, D.C., to prepare for business as usual following his day trip on the Delmarva Peninsula.

How well the president enjoyed his visit to Somerset County that year is unknown, but he found it at least pleasurable enough to return four years later on Labor Day in 1938. This time, President Roosevelt was on official business. His visit was announced well in advance, and hundreds turned out to greet him as he made his way down Main Street via touring car. Crisfield was the kick-off site of the president's whistle-stop train tour of the Eastern Shore that day, and his experience proved memorable. Among the towns and cities he visited on that tour was Salisbury, where he gave a patriotic speech carried nationally by radio.

In that speech, he talked about a "little old lady" he had seen waving an American flag along the roadside, providing a patriotic image of the woman for those listening at home. Days later, the (Baltimore) *Sun* identified that little old lady as Sena Landon, who saluted the president with the flag as his entourage passed an area near her home just outside Hopewell. According to the *Sun*, President Roosevelt was at least the second president to be honored by that flag. Landon said it originally had been waved to celebrate Grover Cleveland's first election to office in 1885.

While Roosevelt's announced visit to Crisfield proved exciting for many, it attracted nowhere near the attention of a future president's visit to the city five years later. In 1943, dancers from John Nelson's Dance Hall on Main Street routinely were bused to Chincoteague Naval Air Base in Virginia to participate in United Service Organizations (USO) shows. Over time one of the dancers, Jackie Sterling, caught the eye of a U.S. Navy pilot named George H.W. Bush, who was training at the base.

In an attempt to impress Sterling, Bush buzzed her house in Crisfield with his plane one afternoon, unaware that a traveling circus was set up nearby. The noise from the airplane scared one of the circus's elephants so badly that it broke free of its bonds and took off through the city! As told years later, the pachyderm ran as fast as an elephant could down Cove Street and onto Asbury Avenue.

Meanwhile, in the Down Neck district just below Crisfield, brothers Cope and Hob Sterling were playing dominoes at the home of their brother, Gord, when Hob excused himself to the outhouse. On his way out of the privy he spied what must have been a

Practically the entire city of Crisfield turned out to see President Franklin D. Roosevelt during his visit on Labor Day 1938. Pictured with the president are senatorial candidate David J. Lewis (center) and Congressman T. Alan Goldsborough.

peculiar sight; an elephant was barreling down the street in his direction. Hob ran to the house, pounded on the door and begged his brothers to let him in, crying out that there was a "heliphant" on the loose, and it was coming to get him!

In reality, the elephant was headed toward a tree with low-hanging branches on which it could scratch its back. It performed the task, then moved on. Its trainer later tracked it to the marshes of Ape's Hole Creek and returned it to the circus grounds. Bush was unofficially grounded at the naval base for his role in the "stampede."

The elephant incident marked the closest Somerset County ever came to facing a military "attack" during World War II. However, nearly all of its residents were touched in one way or another by the war. Thousands of young men from Somerset joined or were drafted into the military and sent overseas. Those who remained on the homefront fought their own war against dwindling resources and fear that their loved ones may never return. The ones who did faced a new era not only in Somerset County, but also in the United States.

Chapter 9

Changing Times

In all, more than two thousand Somerset County men fought in World War II. Among them were members of Crisfield's Company L of the U.S. Army National Guard. Called to active duty in 1941, the unit was transferred to England in 1943 to train for what would become known as the D-Day invasion of Normandy, France. Meanwhile, a new guard unit, Company B, was formed to fill in for Company L as an infantry rifle unit on the homefront.

The war marked changing times in Somerset County. Between rationing everything from sugar to gasoline to meat, blackening vehicle headlights to protect them from enemy sight and participating in air raid drills, women and men who remained in the area had to fill in for the thousands of residents suddenly missing, fighting the war in Europe and Japan. Many did so by working jobs supporting the war effort. Local garment factories made uniforms and tents by the hundreds for military units.

However, perhaps the one Somerset business that shone brightest during World War II was Chas. D. Briddell Inc. By 1945, an estimated 90 percent of the company's business came from military contracts. Most popular among these products for the armed forces were Briddell brand bazooka shells, of which almost two million were produced. The company followed this order with more than one million pry bars and thousands of knives, machetes, grapnels and other military tools.

Throughout the war, Briddell's earned four "E" flags from the U.S. Army and Navy, signifying excellence in product quality and delivery. The war contracts also enabled the company to employ as many as 310 local workers at a time, providing a significant boost to the economy of lower Somerset County.

In northern Somerset, a commodity of quite a different sort was coming into play. Farms, canning companies and forestry operations in Westover and Princess Anne had lost a great deal of production due to the worker shortage caused by the war. Congress responded by giving Somerset County its own internment camp, Camp Somerset, a former National Guard and Civilian Conservation Corps facility five miles south of Princess Anne.

On June 24, 1944, a passenger train made an unscheduled stop in Westover. U.S. soldiers quickly surrounded the train, removed the oak slats nailed across its doors and prepared to unload its cargo: an estimated one thousand German prisoners of war captured following the surrender of the German army in North Africa in 1943. U.S. troops marched the POWs to the thirty-five-acre Camp Somerset, where they were assigned barracks in groups of thirty-eight.

Surrounded by an eight-foot barbed-wire fence, the camp was comprised of six guard towers, thirty-two single-floor barracks, six mess halls, four latrines, two water towers, an infirmary, a recreation building, a sports field and even a dayroom featuring some thirteen hundred German books. It even had indoor plumbing—a luxury some residents of Somerset County still did not have at the time. POWs there were fed daily rations of 3,400 to 3,700 calories each day and were allowed three packs of cigarettes and bottles of beer per week. These items were available at the camp's canteen, which also sold newspapers and magazines.

The POWs were contracted to local farmers, canners and foresters at eight cents per day, a wage far below what those businesses normally would have paid. It was necessary not only for the local economy, but also for the war itself. As the need grew for fruits and vegetables to feed not only families in the United States but soldiers abroad, agriculture in Somerset County returned to heights not seen since the onset of the Great Depression. While the county's average annual agricultural income in the 1930s hovered around $1.5 million, its wartime average skyrocketed to nearly $6 million.

During Camp Somerset's first year, nearly 700 prisoners were assigned to work on local farms. One hundred sixteen were put to work in the county's sawmills, while another 235 worked for independent fruit growers as well as the Somerset Truck Growers Association. Still others were contracted out to help cord timber or clear rights of way for the Eastern Shore Public Service Co.

At least two escapes were recorded at the camp, though the prisoners were quickly recaptured. Escape attempts reportedly increased near the end of the war, as the Germans grew anxious about returning to the section of their native land then controlled by Russia. Records show as many as 1,400 German and Italian POWs were assigned to Camp Somerset by the war's end.

As the POWs were released and American soldiers returned home from the war, Somerset County experienced an industrial growth like none other in the county's history. In 1946, its war contracts largely over, Briddell's returned to production of seafood and ice tools. By that time the company had also expanded into advertising items, such as ashtrays that could be imprinted with a company's name. However, it was clear this would no longer be enough to sustain the company. The seafood industry had dwindled even further, and modern refrigeration practices were making an impact on the sale of ice picks, tongs and chisels.

The company needed a new item. It found one in the form of a letter opener. These letter openers were handcrafted by employee Paul Culver as Christmas presents for the Briddell family. The sleek design reminded the Briddells of a steak knife, and inspiration struck. Within a few months production began on a new line of Briddell steak knives. By the end of 1947 they had a brand name all their own: Carvel Hall. Retailing at $14.95 for a set of six, they quickly became one of the ultimate prestige items in kitchens throughout the United States. Briddell's could not meet the demand.

At the 1951 National Hardware Show alone, Briddell's received more than $1 million in orders for the knives. However, those orders were not to be filled. About five weeks later on March 3, the company's main plant in downtown Crisfield burned to the ground. The Briddells announced they would build a new modern $1 million plant at a location on Route 413 in an area at that time just outside the city limits. As the two-year construction plan commenced, however, retailers found someone else to supply them with Carvel Hall-style knives: overseas manufacturers who copied the Carvel Hall design and were willing to sell it cheaper than Briddell's.

Their chief product stolen out from under them, the Briddells continued to look for new ideas. In 1959 they contracted with the U.S. government to construct mail scooters. However, defects were discovered upon the scooters' delivery, and the repairs cost the company more than it made on the venture. The next year the Briddell family finally gave in, selling the business to the Towle Manufacturing Co. Within six years, Towle had rebuilt the Carvel Hall brand and added new products to the line. In 1967, it changed the name of the company from Chas. D. Briddell Inc. to Carvel Hall. The company remained one of the county's largest employers until the 1980s, when financial difficulty once again set in. It closed in the early 2000s after more than a century in business.

The same year the Briddell plant burned, another industry was making its way to Somerset. Maryland native Edward Piszek founded Mrs. Paul's Kitchens in Philadelphia in 1946, initially selling a line of frozen deviled crab. Within five years, the line had expanded to include frozen fish and other items. Seeking a processing plant closer to the source of that seafood than Philadelphia, he established a factory in Crisfield in 1951, one of four nationwide. The Crisfield plant provided arguably the company's freshest seafood, with oyster shucking and crab picking performed right on the premises. The fresh products were processed, battered, fried and flash frozen and packaged in Crisfield before being sent to Philadelphia for distribution.

By the 1960s, operations at the Crisfield plant expanded beyond just seafood. Employees processed everything from sweet potatoes to apple and corn fritters. In 1976 the last train that ever rumbled out of Crisfield allegedly did so hauling a freight of Mrs. Paul's onion rings.

Things looked good for the Crisfield plant going into the 1980s. The operation employed more than one hundred locally, contributing more than $1 million annually to Crisfield's economy in payroll alone. However, 1982 brought bad news for the local site. Piszek, then sole owner of the company, announced plans to sell Mrs. Paul's to Campbell's Soup. The sale endangered the Crisfield plant's existence. In 1987, the plant processed its last fish portion as operations moved elsewhere.

As the former Briddell company produced cutlery and Mrs. Paul's shipped frozen foods, yet another large industry was seeking a home in Somerset County. In 1873, the Rubber and Celluloid Products Co. was formed in Newark, New Jersey. By 1887, the company had patented a process of creating paintbrushes by securing bristles in rubber. In 1914 its name changed to Rubberset Co. Changing hands throughout the years, it became a division of Sherwin-Williams Co. in 1956. The company's new owner added new products and sought to expand. Unfortunately, that was not an option at the home plant in Newark, so officials scoured the region for a new home.

They found one at the former His-Nibs garment factory on Route 413 just outside what were then the city limits of Crisfield. In 1967, Rubberset moved all U.S. operations—except those on the West Coast—to the Somerset County plant. By 1972 that plant was producing more than eighty-four thousand paintbrushes annually, employing 475 local residents to the annual tune of $3 million. Though no longer one of the county's largest employers, the plant remains in operation today.

While manufacturing played a large part in Somerset County's economy following World War II, it was not the only industry growing in the area. During the war, many farmers in the county began raising chickens. Though wild price fluctuations into the 1960s sometimes made chicken farming a gamble, it paid off for many when the poultry industry became one of the Eastern Shore's largest in the late 1960s and early 1970s. At that time, producers including Perdue Farms and H and H Poultry began guaranteeing prices to growers. Meanwhile, some local entrepreneurs discovered there was more money in industries that supported the poultry industry, like feed production, than there was in actually raising chickens.

Meanwhile, two of Somerset's most traditional industries were still surviving, if not thriving. Businesses like the Hopewell Canning Co., Kings Creek Canning Co. and the John T. Handy Co. helped keep the area's produce-processing industry alive, while the University of Maryland stepped in to assist the seafood industry. In 1954, university officials built a seafood-processing laboratory at Crisfield's Small Boat Harbor to develop new processing procedures as a way to benefit the one hundred twenty-five seafood packinghouses remaining on Maryland's Eastern Shore at that time.

One of the earliest problems the lab's researchers solved was not a question of health, but appearance. When customers of local oysters began noticing red marks on those oysters, business began to decline. Tests at the seafood laboratory proved the discoloration was a natural process and had nothing to do with the oysters' taste, freshness or edibility. Once the public received this information, sales returned to normal.

Throughout the years, scientists at the lab solved many other problems plaguing seafood houses throughout the Eastern Shore and in Southern Maryland. New crab shedding processes developed there helped increase crustacean mortality. A new process for storing crab meat in vacuum-sealed cans helped keep the product fresher longer, allowed consumers nationwide to enjoy crabmeat even in winter. Another process even helped processors get even more meat from crabs, allowing them to more easily extract meat from the crabs' legs, formerly of little use to local packers.

Lab workers also helped raise the status of clams as an Eastern Shore seafood delicacy, developing new sand-filtering procedures. However, perhaps the most notable achievement at the lab was the development of pasteurizing crab meat via microwave radiation, cutting the pasteurization time from nearly two hours to just five minutes and leading to the rise of plastic crabmeat containers in the industry. With the decline of the local seafood industry in the late 1970s and early 1980s, the lab became less and less necessary for local packers. The University of Maryland closed the building's doors for

Businesses like the Hopewell Canning Co., seen here circa 1940, helped keep Somerset County's produce-processing industry alive following World War II.

good in the 1980s, and the state deeded the land to the City of Crisfield, which sold it to a private townhouse developer in 2002.

The same year the university opened its seafood lab in Crisfield, the Somerset County man credited with bringing that education institution to prominence stepped down as its leader. That man, Dr. H.C. "Curley" Byrd, was born "Down Neck" on Feb. 12, 1889. Unlike many boys of the time, Byrd saved most of the money he earned working the water to pay for a college education. He also found plenty of time for recreation. He earned a reputation as Crisfield's first jogger for jogging's sake, and he was a formidable figure on the Crisfield Academy baseball field.

After graduating from the academy in 1905, he left the area to attend Maryland Agricultural College, the institution known today as the University of Maryland. He financed his education with the money he had saved, supplementing it by continuing to work the water on weekends and in the summer. During the school year, he was a member of the university's track team and captain of the school's football team.

But baseball was still Byrd's first love. During his college years he played for semi-professional teams throughout Maryland. After graduation, he signed with the Chicago White Sox in 1910. However, his time with that organization was short, as he was soon traded to a professional team in California, the San Francisco Seals.

While Byrd's athletic prowess allowed him to hold his own in the world of professional baseball, some felt he could do better for himself. In 1912, he heeded that advice and went back to Maryland Agricultural College, this time as an English professor. During this time he began his twenty-one-year career as a football coach for the institution, his 121 career victories earning him Hall of Fame status. In 1921, he helped found the Southern Athletic Conference, and in 1925, the first Curley Byrd Stadium was founded. A new version was dedicated in 1950.

Byrd's accomplishments in collegiate sports were impressive. However, his efforts off the field gave Somerset County even more pride in its native son. In 1920 he helped lead the push to convert the agricultural college into a public university. That year, he became vice president of the new University of Maryland. He would remain in that position until becoming acting president in 1935, then president in 1936.

Media began calling the university "the house that Curley built." Upon his retirement in 1954, that "house" was home to more than twenty-five thousand students, making it the third-largest university in the United States. However, his service to Maryland was not over yet. Following an unsuccessful bid for governor against Theodore McKeldin just six months after his retirement, he served ten years as chairman of the Maryland Tidewater Fisheries Commission, a forerunner of today's Department of Natural Resources.

Byrd passed away October 2, 1970. He was buried in Crisfield's Asbury United Methodist Church Cemetery beneath a tombstone that read: "Harry Clifton 'Curley' Byrd, Educator-Statesman-Conservationist, President Emeritus, Father and Builder of the Greater Consolidated University of Maryland, Founded 1920."

Four years after Byrd's failed gubernatorial bid, another Somerset man succeeded. In 1958 J. Millard Tawes, Crisfield native and Maryland's comptroller for the previous sixteen years, was elected governor of Maryland. Through early 1967, Tawes became one of the most influential leaders in the state's history, taking on environmental issues and helping establish a PBS (Public Broadcasting System) affiliate in Maryland, among other things. President John F. Kennedy lauded him as the first southern governor to support desegregation. His wife Avalynne's famous crab cakes became a staple of the Maryland Pavilion at the 1964–65 World's Fair in New York.

In his hometown, Tawes saw three large-scale projects get off the ground during his time in the governor's mansion. Largely due to the encouragement of John P. Tawes, another Crisfield native and chairman of the Maryland Board of Natural Resources, Crisfield in the 1950s saw construction of a dual highway to replace the stretch of Route 413 running to the city's steamboat wharf and construction of Somers Cove Marina. The state-of-the-art boating facility, proposed as a way to boost the economy of Crisfield and Somerset County, was dedicated on June 16, 1962.

That same year, under Governor Tawes, the state purchased about thirty-six thousand acres of land that had comprised Janes Island, just north of Crisfield with plans to establish Somerset's first state park. Janes Island State Park continues to serve the local community today.

Following two terms in the governor's office, J. Millard Tawes became chairman of the Board of Natural Resources from 1967 to 1969. He then became the first leader of the Maryland Department of Natural Resources, serving in that capacity until 1971. In 1977 an inaugural crab and clambake was held in Tawes's honor to help

Maryland Governor J. Millard Tawes, seen here with his wife, Avalynne, was one of the state's most influential political leaders.

The rustic Crisfield area workshop of renowned decoy carvers Lem and Steve Ward drew visitors from around the world. *Courtesy Scorchy Tawes.*

raise money for construction of a proposed J. Millard Tawes Museum. Tawes saw only two of the annual events prior to his death on June 25, 1979. Now sponsored by the Crisfield Area Chamber of Commerce, the J. Millard Tawes Crab and Clam Bake has become Somerset County's largest annual one-day tourism event and a mainstay of the Maryland political scene, held each July at Somers Cove Marina, adjacent to the museum that bears Tawes's name.

Two more lower Somerset residents also gained prominence following World War II. The famous Ward Brothers, Lem and Steve, were born in 1896 and 1895, respectively, in the Down Neck district below Crisfield. In the 1910s, the Ward Brothers taught themselves to carve decoys as a way to make money for their family. They earned a degree of perfectionism from their father, Travis, a boatbuilder and barber. By the 1920s they had become the area's premier carvers, making decoys real enough to fool hunters, as well as ducks and geese. Between carving and barbering, the siblings made a decent living. Decoys were \$1.25 each, haircuts 15¢.

Unfortunately, both industries would decline in the 1930s as the waterfowl population dwindled and the Great Depression left many without the spare change for a decent haircut. It was then that the Ward Brothers decided to dedicate their time to decorative decoy carving. In 1948 their carvings won the National Decoy Contest in New York, bringing them nationwide acclaim. Throughout the years their business, L.T. Ward and

Crisfield's first National Hard Crab Derby in 1948 sparked a tradition that remains in the early twenty-first century. Pictured, from left, are Rob Wharton, Wilbert "Scobie" Coulbourne and Naugie Adams. *Photo by Dick Moore, courtesy Scorchy Tawes.*

Bro.—Wildfowl Counterfeiters in Wood, located in a small workshop beside their birth home, drew visitors from around the world.

Despite the popularity of their work, they refused to raise prices beyond what they felt was fair market value, even as sales of their past carvings on the secondary market reached into the hundreds of dollars. In 1968 the Ward Foundation was organized in Salisbury as a non-profit educational organization to memorialize the master carvers. The next year while filling their largest order ever, $70,000 worth of decoys for Delaware industrialist William DuPont, both siblings suffered health setbacks, Lem a paralyzing stroke and Steve cataracts. These conditions prohibited them from producing more than eleven of the seventy decoys DuPont ordered. They would be the last birds the duo would carve.

Steve Ward died seven years later in 1976. Lem followed in 1984. However, their memories live on today. The Crisfield Heritage Foundation has preserved the old Ward workshop in Crisfield and includes it on its summer tours. The Ward Foundation opened the Ward Museum of Wildfowl Art in Salisbury and now operates the facility in affiliation with Salisbury University. It also sponsors an annual worldwide carving competition in the Wards' name in Ocean City. Ward carvings remain the most popular among decoy collectors today, with prices in the tens of thousands of dollars.

While Somerset leaders like Byrd, Tawes and the Ward Brothers were hitting their stride following World War II, others sought new ways to honor the county's heritage. In 1947 the *Crisfield Times* published an editorial suggesting a hard crab derby be held, emulating the Kentucky Derby and other popular races of the day. The first National Hard Crab Derby was held in front of the Crisfield Post Office the next year as crabs were placed in the center of a circle. The first one to the circle's edge was the winner.

The derby gained even more steam in 1950, when it was held in connection with the Chesapeake Bay Fishing Fair, based that year in Crisfield. A street parade, art and industrial fair, and Miss Crisfield beauty pageant (the forerunner to the next year's Miss Crustacean pageant) were added to make the crab races an even bigger attraction. Today sponsored by the Crisfield Area Chamber of Commerce and American Legion Post 16 every Labor Day weekend in Somers Cove Marina, crab races have evolved into a four-hundred-crustacean affair complete with a specially designed track. The National Hard Crab Derby is now known throughout the United States, thanks in large part to coverage in such publications as *National Geographic* and television programs including *The Mike Douglas Show* and *Late Night with David Letterman.*

A decade after the founding of the Crab Derby, Princess Anne's annual signature festival, Olde Princess Anne Days, was formed in 1958.

A nod to the town's 1700's roots, the October event features a tour of some of the county's most historic homes, interweaving historical reenactments such as fox hunts and period musical performances.

The Deal Island Skipjack Races, discussed in chapter seven, are held each Labor Day. An 1800s Festival in Fairmount similarly pays tribute to the history of that area every Memorial Day weekend.

Even as these festivals were being founded, however, the area was beginning to lose the traditions on which they were based. The seafood industry was at an all-time low and sinking fast. In 1957, one of the trade's most notable figures, Annie White Parkinson Nelson, passed away. Better known as Crabbin' Annie, Parkinson was born in Deal Island about 1900. She was a single mother of five by the time she moved to Crisfield in 1929.

Her first foray into the seafood business came about the same time, when she got a job at an area shucking house to help pay her twelve-dollar monthly mortgage and put food on the table. Soon she gave up shucking in favor of crabbing. Operating a crab-shedding operation from her backyard and selling crabs from her West Main Street home, she earned a living for more than two decades as a female pioneer in what was largely deemed a man's business.

Natural disasters also continued to impact the area. Chief among them was Hurricane Hazel. Named by many as the worst disaster in the history of Somerset County, the storm blew in the morning of October 15, 1954. Nearly the entire county took a direct hit. Coastal areas including Crisfield, Smith Island and Deal Island never stood a chance. Once the storm had passed, residents toured the area, surveying damage that ranged from the collapse of roofs on some buildings to the entire destruction of others.

Local schoolchildren performed a play in front of the Somerset County Courthouse as part of Olde Princess Anne Days festivities in 1959.

The 1959 Olde Princess Anne Days celebration included carriage rides, seen here in front of the Arcade Theater.

Hurricane Hazel ravaged the docks at Crisfield's steamboat wharf in 1954. The storm caused massive damage in nearly every part of Somerset County.

Two days of gale-force winds and exceptionally high tides caused $20 million in damages throughout the Delmarva Peninsula in March 1962. The flooding rose above the foundation of Roger Hoffman's store in Deal Island, seen here. *Courtesy Faye Pianka.*

Less than a decade later, on March 6 and 7, 1962, Somerset again became the target of Mother Nature as two low-pressure systems merged off the coast, creating gale-force winds and causing tides to swell as much as nine feet above normal. Smith Island became submerged, and the streets of Crisfield, Deal Island and other coastal Somerset areas were flooded with water. While the storm certainly made its mark on Somerset, the county got off easy compared to surrounding areas. Property in the beach resorts of Maryland, Delaware and Virginia eroded overnight, and the wind and waves toppled many buildings. President John F. Kennedy declared Worcester County a disaster area. In all, the storm caused an estimated $20 million in damages throughout the Delmarva Peninsula.

By the 1960s, Somerset was beginning to face not only economic pressures, but social ones, as well. In 1963, race-based riots in Cambridge, in Dorchester County, made national headlines. Tensions throughout the Eastern Shore continued to run high into 1964, when African American students at Maryland State College began protesting against discrimination at restaurants in Princess Anne. Owners of many of those restaurants tentatively had agreed to end segregationist policies following the Cambridge riots, but not all held true to their word.

Forming the Student Appeal For Equality (SAFE), the affected students prompted town commissioners to form the Princess Anne Biracial Commission, which encouraged desegregation in the town's restaurants. On February 21, approximately forty African American students tested the commission's progress by dividing into groups and requesting service at each of the town's six restaurants. Only two, Eddie's restaurant and the Washington Hotel, obliged.

The next day, student leader John Wilson attempted to enter Tull's Restaurant, where the group had been refused service, and was beaten by three restaurant patrons. The students were moved to action, marching on Tull's and becoming involved in a fight that led to three arrests. Two days after the march, a cross was burned on the college's football practice field. The home of Wilson's uncle, Princess Anne resident Leon Gates, was also bombed.

Princess Anne town officials requested additional support from the Maryland State Police and later the National Guard to help curb additional violence. Talks with the Biracial Commission broke down, and against the encouragement of Maryland State College President J.T. Williams to solve the problem peacefully through established channels, the students once again took matters into their own hands.

On February 26, Cambridge civil rights leader Gloria Richardson headed a march of more than three hundred students down the streets of Princess Anne, where they held a sit-in to block traffic. An estimated one hundred state troopers descended upon the demonstration with dogs and fire hoses, chasing the demonstrators back to the campus under a barrage of bricks and bottles. Twenty-seven were arrested.

The events in Princess Anne drew the attention of national civil rights leaders, including comedian Dick Gregory and Student Non-Violent Action Committee President John Lewis, who gave public speeches in the town advocating the desegregation of not only Princess Anne, but also the entire Eastern Shore. That March, thirty students from

Maryland State College met with Governor Tawes, who vowed to encourage Somerset County's inclusion in Maryland's public accommodations law.

While Somerset was eventually included in that law, the fight was far from over. Reacting to the news, restaurant owners from Princess Anne to Crisfield hung signs in their windows reiterating the fact that they reserved the right to refuse service to anyone, especially African Americans and their supporters. Some even listed Tawes by name.

The Ku Klux Klan and National States Rights Party, both white supremacist organizations, also joined in the fray, attempting to recruit new members in Somerset County. In August 1966, the States Rights Party attempted to hold a rally on the steps of the Somerset County Courthouse, but were blocked by Maryland Circuit Court Judge E. McMaster Duer. Party members fought the injunction to the U.S. Supreme Court, where it was ultimately dismissed.

Student demonstrations moved from the streets of Princess Anne to the campus of Maryland State College, where 178 were arrested during an April 1970 demonstration demanding Williams's resignation. He obliged them that August after having overseen the college for twenty-three years.

By 1968 Somerset had indeed become part of Maryland's public accommodations law, requiring massive changes in many areas, not the least of which was the county's school system. In the late 1960s, Somerset County boasted six high schools: Washington, Crisfield, Marion and Deal Island for Caucasian students, and Somerset and Woodson for African Americans. Under pressure to desegregate its schools by the 1969–1970 school year, the Somerset County Board of Education proposed what its members hoped would be the perfect solution: a central high school for all Somerset students located in Princess Anne.

However, the plan did not bear fruit. Instead of being lauded for their forward thinking, board members were attacked by communities throughout the county. The high schools, along with local churches, were the hubs of most Somerset communities, and no one wanted theirs taken away. In the end, the board compromised, consolidating Marion and Woodson High Schools at Crisfield High, and Deal Island and Somerset High Schools at Washington High.

Early 1972 saw another crisis for at least two schools in Somerset County. On January 23, 1972, two classrooms at the old Woodson High School, which had served as a middle school since fall 1969, were burned by arsonists in a morning fire. On February 2, arsonists struck again, this time at Crisfield High School, which was comprised of two buildings on Somerset Avenue. The fire destroyed the older of the two, which had been constructed in 1926. A new Crisfield High School, incorporating part of the property's newer building, constructed in 1953, was opened in 1973 and still stands as the only high school in lower Somerset County. No arrests were made in either fire.

In 1998 the idea of a central high school for Somerset was raised again, this time not for desegregation purposes, but for budget concerns. The proposal saw similar reaction to its 1968 predecessor. Amid protests coming predominately from the county's southern end, the board passed a vote to create a central high school, then retracted it following a public referendum and election that saw most of the proposal's supporters voted out of office. Eventually a plan was passed that would allow the county's high schools to remain open, but centrally combine its middle schools and close longstanding elementary schools in Westover, Marion Station and Crisfield.

A diminishing population was paramount to both the 1968 and 1998 school closing proposals. According to the 1930 U.S. Census, more than tweny-three thousand people inhabited Somerset County. By 1970 that number had dropped to just under nineteen thousand. Though the area continued to receive national recognition—the unique Cheops time capsule developed in Crisfield for America's bicentennial drew financial support from U.S. Senator Barry Goldwater and accolades from President Jimmy Carter and Queen Elizabeth II of England, among others—its population continued to dwindle through the 1990s.

One problem was a lack of jobs in the area as the seafood and agricultural industries continued to dwindle. In the early 1980s state officials proposed a solution—but it was not immediately popular. A new state prison proposed in Westover could provide hundreds of jobs in Somerset and surrounding areas while helping solve the problem of overcrowded prisons elsewhere in the state, they thought. Many Somerset residents immediately rebuffed the idea, fearing for their safety in case of an escape and wondering whether most of the promised jobs would go to local residents or if employees would be imported from Baltimore and other areas.

Regardless of the outcry, state officials moved forward with the plan, and Eastern Correctional Institution (ECI) opened in Westover in 1987. Two decades later, the facility is one of the county's two largest employers, vying annually with the University of Maryland Eastern Shore for the top spot.

ECI's inaugural year marked a particularly difficult time for Somerset's economy. While this large new employer was moving in, operations ceased at the Crisfield plant of Mrs. Paul's Kitchens and were scaled back at Carvel Hall, creating a sudden glut of unemployment. Little did local officials know things were about to get even worse.

The evening of November 11, 1987, a U.S. Coast Guard boat was returning to its Crisfield station near Somers Cove Marina after towing a disabled vessel to Crisfield when its crew spotted what looked like a fire on the city's coast. A crewmember radioed Somerset County Emergency Services, which immediately received a second call from a civilian who confirmed the fire was at the lumberyard of J.P. Tawes and Bro. Hardware. The Crisfield Volunteer Fire Department was dispatched at 10:40 p.m.

Firefighters arrived to find the forty-eight-thousand-square-foot lumberyard engulfed in flames. Strong winds threatened a firestorm as flames shot more than one hundred feet in the air. Marion Station firefighters were immediately called for assistance and were on the scene by 10:50 p.m. They reported seeing light from the blaze as far away as their own firehouse seven miles away. As the fire spread to adjacent buildings, more calls for assistance were issued. Firefighters from Princess Anne and New Church, Atlantic and Greenbackville, Virginia, arrived, as did a foam truck from NASA's Wallops Island Flight Facility in Accomack County. By 11:30 p.m., U.S. Coast Guard cutter *Chokeberry* had been called in to supply eight lines of water to the fire trucks, by then surrounding more than one full block of downtown Crisfield.

As the fire spread farther, another call for assistance went out, bringing firefighters from Salisbury, Fruitland, Allen and Parsonsburg. With eleven fire departments plus the Coast Guard fighting the blaze through the night, officials finally had the fire under control by 4:30 a.m. October 12. By dawn the landscape of Crisfield had changed forever, with eleven buildings destroyed or so heavily damaged they had been marked for immediate demolition. The burned businesses suddenly threw even more into Somerset County's unemployment ranks. The fire was ruled an arson.

The events of 1987 plunged Somerset into a recession from which it would not even begin to emerge until the early twenty-first century. In 2001, Maryland delegate Charles McClenahan proposed a ferry between Crisfield and Point Lookout in St. Mary's County as a way to embolden the Somerset economy by funneling more visitors through the area.

By that time Somerset had already cast its lot as a tourism destination, promoting historical tours of Princess Anne, Crisfield and Smith Island. Daytrip cruises from Crisfield to Smith and Tangier Islands had steadily increased in popularity since the 1970s. The Library of Congress Folklife Field School captured Crisfield's economic progression from the maritime industry to the tourism industry during a study of the area in 2003. It presented its findings during the 2004 Smithsonian Folklife Festival in Washington, D.C., which featured Crisfield and other changing maritime communities in the United States.

St. Mary's officials did not share McClenahan's vision for the Chesapeake Bay shuttle to Point Lookout, but that did not mean the end of the ferry proposal. In 2003 McClenahan's successor, Delegate D. Page Elmore, and other legislators took up the cause, changing the destination to Reedville in Northumberland County, Virginia. This, they surmised, could help increase traffic through both areas, which dead-ended for street traffic at the water's edge. The proposal made regional headlines as elected officials endeavored to return ferry service to the Chesapeake Bay for the first time in decades.

The proposal became mired in a series of expensive years-long feasibility studies. As of winter 2007, no infrastructure work had yet been done on any ferries or landing sites. More than half a decade after it was first proposed, however, Somerset County had seen one economic side effect of the non-existent ferry. News of the proposal quickly piqued the interest of condominium and townhouse developers, who before had not been aware of the abundance of undeveloped waterfront property throughout the county.

Almost overnight the county was besieged with proposals for upscale waterfront residential developments. In Crisfield, city council members jumped at the opportunity to put land that had sat vacant since the 1970s back on the tax rolls. Much of the property proposed for development belonged to the city, anyway, as the result of foreclosures throughout the years. City officials partnered with a private advisory and sales group, Crisfield Associates LLC, to steer development and help sell surplus property.

However, many residents of Crisfield disliked the partnership, claiming it could be used to sell off or develop public venues, including Somers Cove Marina and the City Dock, so the city and Crisfield Associates could make a fast buck. Voters replaced the

Crisfield's landmark ice plant was demolished as condominiums rose above the horizon in March 2004. The onslaught of waterfront construction that followed changed the city's skyline and symbolized the area's economic transition in the early twenty-first century.

mayor and nearly the entire city council during elections in 2006, and the new council quickly voided the city's agreement with Crisfield Associates.

Regardless, condominium developers continued to swoop into Crisfield. Between 2003 and 2006, the city's population swelled from 2,500 to more than 3,500, with predictions that it would keep growing. It anchored a population boom in the county that saw similar increases in Princess Anne and outlying areas throughout the region. At the same time, property values suddenly skyrocketed. With state assessments issued in 2005, some property owners saw values—and essentially the amount they would be forced to pay in property taxes—increase by as much as 600 percent.

Local homes worth $50,000 before 2001 suddenly went on the market for five times that price. That same year, the land that once housed Mrs. Paul's Kitchen sold for more than $10 million, a new record. Many were seeking to cash in. By late 2006, however, the sales boom leveled off. Property still sold for much more than it had just five years prior, but the astonishing increase in prices seen between 2003 and early 2006 finally tapered off.

Two centuries after it was first charted by Captain John Smith, Somerset County has seen a tremendous amount of history, from the American Revolution of the 1770s to the Civil Rights Movement of the 1960s. Its people have helped shape the region, the state and in some cases even the nation. Through it all, Somerset has persevered, continuing its existence as one of the true gems of Maryland's Eastern Shore.

Bibliography

"At Princess Anne." *Time*, October 30, 1933.

Charles, Alfred D. "Eastern Shore Reception One of Contrasts." *Baltimore Sun*. Baltimore, MD, September 6, 1938.

"Colored People Celebrate." *Crisfield Times*. Crisfield, MD, August 1, 1914.

"County News Letters." *Crisfield Times*. Crisfield, MD, July 7, 1917.

———. *Crisfield Times*. Crisfield, MD, September 1, 1917.

———. *Crisfield Times*. Crisfield, MD, December 8, 1917.

Davidson, Thomas E., and Helen C. Rountree. *Eastern Shore Indians of Virginia and Maryland*. Charlottesville: University Press of Virginia, 1997.

Democrat and News. Cambridge, MD, July 20, 1901.

Earle, Swepson. *Chesapeake Bay Country*. Baltimore: Thomsen-Ellis Co., 1923.

Evans, Ben. *Memories of Steamboats, Campmeetings, Skipjacks and Islands of the Chesapeake Bay*. Princess Anne, MD: Marylander and Herald, 1977.

"Foreigner Sees Crisfield." *Crisfield Times*. Crisfield, MD, February 25, 1911.

Hall, Marion. *The History of Oriole and Its Satellites*. 1964.

Hartzler, Daniel D. *A Band of Brothers: Photographic Epilogue to Marylanders in the Confederacy*. New Windsor, MD: Bookcrafters, 1992.

"Hon. John W. Crisfield" (obituary). *Salisbury Advertiser*. Salisbury, MD, January 16, 1897.

Hornberger, Patrick, and Linda Turbyville. *Forgotten Beacons: The Lost Lighthouses of the Chesapeake Bay*. Trappe, MD: Eastwind Publishing, 1997.

Jopling, Carol F. *Churches of Somerset County, Maryland*. Annapolis: The Annapolis Publishing Co., 2000.

Mann, Hunter R., III. "Blaze Incinerates Two-Block Area of Crisfield." *Firehouse*. Boulder, CO, January 1988.

Mariner, Kirk. *True Tales of the Eastern Shore*. New Church, VA: Miona Publications, 2003.

Maryland's Historic Somerset. Princess Anne, MD: Somerset County Board of Education, 1955.

"Mayor Richardson Gets Big Contract." *Crisfield Times*. Crisfield, MD, June 30, 1917.

Mowbray, William W. *The Eastern Shore Baseball League*. Centreville, MD: Tidewater Publishers, 1989.

Newman, Harry W. *Maryland and the Confederacy*. Annapolis, 1976.

O'Connor, Jean Callaghan. *Camp Somerset and Camp Easton: German POW Camps on the Eastern Shore 1943–1946*. 1994.

"One Hundred Years of Crisfield Memories." *Crisfield Times*. Crisfield, MD, February 25, 2004.

Plummer, Norman H. *Maryland's Oyster Navy: The First Fifty Years*. St. Michaels, MD: Chesapeake Bay Maritime Museum, 1993.

Preston, Dickson J. *Newspapers of Maryland's Eastern Shore*. Centreville, MD: Tidewater Publishers, 1986.

Pyle, Howard. "A Peninsular Canaan." *Harper's New Monthly Magazine* 59, no. 349. New York: Harper and Brothers, June 1879.

"Rescuer Reported Dead." *Baltimore Sun*. Baltimore, February 8, 1936.

Riggin, Gordon E., and Gordon Ruark. "Fire Sweeps Business Area of Crisfield." *Baltimore Sun*. Baltimore, March 31, 1928.

Scott, Walter. "Personality Parade." *Parade*, April 23, 1989.

Shomette, Donald G. *Pirates on the Chesapeake: Being a True History of Pirates, Picaroons, and Raiders on Chesapeake Bay 1610–1807*. Centreville, MD: Tidewater Publishers, 1985.

Stump, Brice Neal. *Somerset County: A Pictorial History*. Norfolk, VA: The Donning Company Publishers, 1985.

Toomey, Daniel Carroll. *Marylanders at Gettysburg*. Baltimore: H.G. Roebuck and Son, Inc., 1994.

Torrence, Clayton. *Old Somerset on the Eastern Shore of Maryland: A Study in Foundations and Founders*. Richmond: Whittet and Shepperson, 1935.

Touart, Paul Baker. *Somerset: An Architectural History*. Baltimore: Collins Lithographing, Inc. Maryland Historical Trust, 1990.

"U.S. Dreadnought in the Crisfield Harbor." *Crisfield Times*. Crisfield, MD, February 24, 1917.

Ward, Gus. *Down in Maryland*. Federalsburg, MD: J.W. Stowell Printing Co., 1929.

Wennersten, John R. *The Oyster Wars of Chesapeake Bay*. Centreville, MD: Tidewater Publishers, 1981.

———. *Tidewater Somerset 1850–1970*. Princess Anne, MD: 1976.

Williamson, Gene. *Guns on the Chesapeake: The Winning of America's Independence*. Bowie, MD: Heritage Books, Inc., 1998.

Wilson, Woodrow T. *Crisfield, Maryland 1676–1976*. Baltimore: Gateway Press, Inc., 1977.

———. *History of Crisfield and Surrounding Areas on Maryland's Eastern Shore*. Baltimore: Gateway Press, Inc., 1973.

———. *Quindocqua, Maryland: Indian Country*. Baltimore: Gateway Press, Inc., 1980.

———. *Thirty-Four Families of Old Somerset County, Maryland*. Baltimore: Gateway Press, Inc., 1977.